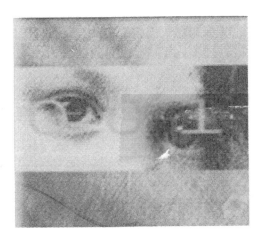

That's Customer Focus!

*The Overworked and
Under-appreciated Manager's
Guide to Creating a Customer-
Focused Organization*

F. Ray Miller
Laura E. Miller

Dedication

This book is dedicated to all those committed to making a difference.

We would also like to thank those, oh so many companies who continue to deliver mediocre and poor service.

Your lack of customer focus continues to provide so many great stories and examples of what not to do for our books and training programs.

More importantly, we would like to thank those truly customer-focused organizations.

You are an inspiration and living proof that this stuff really works.

"There is only one boss. The customer. And he (or she) can fire everybody in the company from the chairman on down, simply by spending his (or her) money somewhere else."

Sam Walton

Visit www.booksurge.com to order additional copies.

E-mail: support@thatscustomerfocus.com
Telephone: 1(416) 698-8230

Table of Contents

Table of Contents

Foreword

We wrote this book because we wanted to help you implement an essential business strategy which will make your business **more profitable, period**.

We realize, there is a better than 80% chance, that there are many times when you feel under-appreciated and over-worked. And if that's the case, there is a good chance that your employees feel this way as well.

Let's face it, your days are filled with dealing with problems, reports and those pesky customer or employee problems. Time is something you don't have a lot of, and while you know deep down that improving customer focus and service in your organization would be good for business, for some reason you just haven't been able to do it. The good news is you bought this book.

Let's very quickly review the **number one reason** why creating a customer-focused organization is good for you and your business.

Your Company will be more profitable. This happens in a couple of ways. First, truly customer-focused companies have loyal customers. They buy more, they cost less to serve because they know your processes, they tell you when things go wrong so you can fix the problems and they tell their friends, family and associates about how great you are and as a result you get more customers. Harvard Business Review conducted a study a while back and determined that a 5% increase in customer loyalty will positively impact your bottom line by between 25% and 125% depending on your type of business.

Also, truly customer-focused companies are more productive. Employees are motivated, and perform their jobs more effectively. Re-work, duplication of effort and mistakes are significantly reduced. These all cost you money in terms of time spent, money spent, loss of productivity and loss of business. Your turnover also reduces so you keep your staff longer and don't experience down-time, productivity losses and employee morale related issues.

This book will help you to get started on the road to creating or enhancing customer focus in your organization, department or business. We have provided you with explanations, examples, tools and exercises which will help you to create customer focus. We know that you are time compressed. That's probably why you bought this book rather than attend some training program. So, we have attempted to filter out theoretical concepts and focus our attention on specific steps and actions which you can take.

We have spent the last 20 years working with companies to help them enhance their service delivery and improve their customer focus. Some have been very successful at doing this while others didn't quite get there. Commitment, strategic thinking, targeted actions and hard work are required if you are to be successful.

What we have covered in this book are really the nuts and bolts of creating customer focus. Becoming truly customer-focused takes time, however, if you implement what we cover in this book, you will see significant improvements.

Foreword

Just a few comments about the way this book is structured. Each Chapter contains an introduction page which also includes a description of the objectives of the chapter and some discussion concerning why the topic is important.

You will also see an icon like this | *Action* | quite often. This indicates specific action steps that you can take related to the topic being discussed.

Included in this book are several exercises designed to help you implement what is presented. Some of these exercises include worksheets. We have created a PDF downloadable file which contains all of these forms and tools. You can download these for free by going to www.thatscustomerfocus.com/downloads/forms.htm .

As an alternative you may wish to photocopy these rather than write in you book. Other exercises don't require worksheets but I suggest that you have a notepad and pen nearby so you can capture any ideas, observations and inspirations.

In the final chapter of this book we have also provided you with a Critical Action Items checklist to help you organize and develop your Customer-Focused Strategy and Plan. Again, you may wish to make a photocopy of these pages.

One last thing before we get started: why not take a couple of minutes and develop a list of the reasons why you want to create a Customer Focus in your Company, Department or Business. Why not take a moment to jot down your thoughts. Then refer to this list from time to time to remind yourself of why you are doing this and the pay-offs you want to achieve.

"Luck is where preparation meets opportunity. I wish you the best of luck."

Customer Focus 101

Chapter 1

It's pretty safe to assume that you intrinsically know that creating a customer focus is important. The fact that you bought this book is a good sign. We could jump right into step-by-step instructions, a recipe if you will, for getting the job done. But here's the thing: you could try baking a cake by following the recipe, but without understanding the basics of cooking there's a really good chance it won't turn out like in the picture. You could try building a car, but without a fundamental understanding of mechanical engineering, would you want to drive it down the highway at 60 miles an hour? Would you build a house without a fundamental understanding of construction, legal issues and financing? Probably not.

So, before you can take on the task of creating a customer-focused culture, there are a number of fundamentals you need to be crystal clear about regarding service quality, the financial consequences of a customer-focused strategy, and the impact customer expectations and perceptions have on your business. Let's take a few minutes to review these.

This chapter:

- defines what service is and is NOT
- discusses why service is important and presents a business case for creating a Customer-Focused Organization
- provides you with tools to create a business case for your specific organization
- explores customer expectations and customer perceptions when it comes to service

Why is this important?

If our introduction to this chapter hasn't convinced you, consider this:

> **An alarmingly high number of service improvement or customer-focus initiatives fail miserably, despite the best intentions of all those involved.**

There are many reasons for this failure, most of which can be traced back to management. Some organizations try to copy what another organization has done, yet it doesn't work. It's easy to copy steps and procedures; but without understanding the mind-set and thinking of those who originated the processes, you will never achieve the same outcomes. Successful customer-focused organizations all share a similar mind-set regarding what service is and is not.

Let's explore this further.

Customer Focus 101

What Service Is and Is Not

It has been our experience that stories and parables are the best teachers. They help us to personally identify with someone else's pain, frustration, surprise and delight. We use stories frequently in our training programs and we hear many stories from our participants. The following two stories help illustrate what service is Not.

Like many of you, I have become a slave to technology. While I am developing a certain degree of comfort with most types of technology such as computers, pda's, vcr's, cd/dvd players and lcd's I almost always have a sense of trepidation whenever I encounter a problem with anything commonly identified by three initials. I was having a problem with a new "pda" and went back to the store that sold it to me, hoping for some "expert" help.

There appeared to be only one sales representative available so I had to wait for what seemed like an eternity. Finally it was my turn for help. The attendant was very approachable and friendly. I recognized him as the person that had served me a week earlier. He smiled and asked how he could help me. The first thing out of my mouth was "I bought this pda here a week ago and as a matter of fact you served me." I continued to outline my problem in my own clear but non-techno-speak way. As I spoke, the attendant continued to smile and seemed to be listening, that is until he asked me his first question which was, "Did you buy that item here?" Again, he continued to smile and asked more ridiculous questions like did I have my receipt? And did I follow the set-up instructions properly? The harder he smiled the angrier I got. In the end, the solution to my problem was that I would have to visit the manufacturer's web site and if I couldn't find the information there, I would need to contact their support desk. But that's a story for another time. I actually left the store extremely angry because I had come to the conclusion that my smiling attendant was really enjoying ticking me off. Why else would he be smiling so hard yet be so unhelpful?

Service is not merely someone who smiles and says, "Thank you."

In my job I get to travel quite a bit. Finding a good meal in some places can be a bit of a challenge. But sometimes when you are hungry you can't be too picky. On one particular occasion I was very hungry and happened across a fast food steak house. The building looked like a big green barn. Upon entering the restaurant you see huge photographs of sumptuous meals each assigned their own unique identifying number. It amazes me how what one gets on one's plate never looks as good as the photos but when one is hungry, sacrifices are made.

This particular restaurant was set up cafeteria style. You would pick up a tray, put it on the rail, place your order with a cashier, pay for your meal, get the meal handed to you and then you would find a seat. The cashier serving me was required to repeat my order into a microphone attached to the cash register station so now the entire world knew what I was having for dinner.

I placed the following order: "I will have a number 4, well done, baked potato with sour cream, salad bar, a diet coke and no dessert please." I knew the cashier got my order correctly because she repeated it word for word into the microphone. The first thing the cashier asked me was. "Would you like dessert with you meal?" I said "I know you know I don't want dessert because you said so when you placed my order. Right?" She said "Yes sir." So I asked, "Why did you ask me if I wanted dessert?" She said "I have to sir." I asked her why. She said "It's step 7." I inquired "Step 7?" She said "Yes sir. Step 7. We pride ourselves on following all the steps to customer service here sir. Asking the customer if they want dessert is step 7."

*She reached down and grabbed a clipboard which had in red bold words, **The 10 Steps to Customer Service**. And indeed it was true that Step 7 was "Ask customer if they want dessert with their meal."*

Customer Focus 101

So I said to her, Since you knew I didn't want dessert, why did you ask me?" She said, "I have to sir." I asked "What would happen if you didn't ask?" She said "I'd get in trouble sir." So I asked "Does that make sense to you?" She said "No sir, but they do lots of things here that don't make any sense, but I need this job." She then went on to tell me about some of the other things that she and her colleagues had to do in the name of service that would astound you.

Service is not a series of steps that are required to be performed with every customer.

Service is adding People to your Product.

There is a huge difference between the **Service** you provide and the **Services** you offer…don't confuse them!

Too often, people confuse the services a company offers with the quality of service that it provides. There is a difference between service and services. Valet parking at a hotel, financial transactions at a bank, delivery of goods by a retailer and safety inspections by utilities are examples of services provided. Simply put, services are the "stuff" that organizations offer their customers. If your car is not brought to you quickly and in the same condition as you left it, if the ATM machine isn't working or eats your card, if your goods are not delivered when promised, this stuff is sub-par and customers react in the same way as they would if the product they purchased did not function as it was supposed to. Great services without great service from customer-contact staff will leave a bad memory.

Service is the quality measure of how an organization delivers the "stuff." Service is a people dimension.

Service is an attitude and belief shared by every employee that the customer is most important.

Below are some firsthand experiences from participants in our *Customers Forever* workshop.

Katrina, **Chemical Engineer**	*"One of my worst experiences was at a hair salon. I asked for a permanent and a new coloring and the hair dresser did a terrible job. It was obvious she was trying to handle too many customers at once. The cut was too short, the coloring uneven and the perm was too tight. When I complained to the salon manager she said, "Well, we're very busy. Besides, it doesn't look that bad." There was absolutely no attempt to even hear my complaint much less do something about it!"*
John, **Landscape Design**	*"My experience was actually kind of funny. My buddy and I went to one of those mega home improvement centers. I needed some fasteners to fix a cabinet. It was just a few small items to fix a broken latch. When the cashier tried to ring it up, the scanner on the cash register wouldn't scan the bar code.* *"I can't ring this up. There's no SKU number," he said. His tone sounded like he was accusing me of doing something wrong.* *"I don't know the SKU number," I said, half laughingly.* *"Well, what am I suppose to do?" he asked. His attitude was incredible.* *"How about calling a manager for help?" I said (half shocked now).* *"Can't you just get a different one?" he suggested.* *"No, but I can go to a different store." I said. Then I left.*

Customer Focus 101

Good service comes from actions which make the customer experience with your company one which exceeds his or her expectations. It is the...

- Attitude
- Care
- Helpfulness
- Responsiveness
- Courtesy
- Knowledge
- Reliability
- Concern
- Enthusiasm
- Expertise

...that people bring to their jobs in the delivery of "the stuff" for which they are responsible.

Service quality requires the **enthusiastic participation of every employee** in every aspect of the service effort. Relying on the product, technology, professional services or "stuff" to impress the customer, leaves too much to chance.

Why Service is Important

Research from a litany of reliable sources tells us that the primary reason that customers switch their loyalty from one company to another, in the range of 40% to 68%, is because of a perceived attitude of indifference on the part of the service provider. Sure, some leave because of price, or product quality, or other personal reasons; but the vast majority leave because of Poor Service.

These days, customers are really in the driver's seat. The options and choices of similar products at similar prices at similar quality levels are greater than ever. Advances in technology, reductions in production time and access to global distribution mean that products and services can be duplicated and customized faster than ever before. And your customers know this!

Consumers have more choices than ever before. This creates an interesting challenge. How do you create value when customers today are not seeing much difference in the choices they are offered?

Customers tend to look at value from four perspectives. The **Price** of the product or service, the **Quality** of the product or service, the degree of **Innovation** offered by the product and the **Service** provided to customers.

The quality of products continues to improve universally and competitors have developed the ability to duplicate even the most complex of those products. Innovation attracts younger consumers but no sooner do we see one innovation, than someone else comes along and clones it plus adds a few more bells and whistles. Consider the evolution of the flat screen LCD TV. A couple of years ago, few could afford such a luxury item. Now there are LCD TVs to fit a wide range of budgets. And in addition to the traditional manufacturers of televisions, it seems that any one who manufactures computers also has their own LCD TV. Developing a competitive advantage based solely on product quality and/or innovation is very difficult. And sustaining it is very expensive. You will also find that there is more price parity today than ever before. Very few companies can compete for long using price as a differentiating factor. By shifting your emphasis to service quality, you will find the greatest room for differentiation.

Customer Focus 101

For most companies, customer loyalty is the key to future profitability and growth. Corporate newsletters, national periodicals, and most executive speeches are peppered with a litany of examples demonstrating the relationship between customer loyalty and profitability. In almost every market we've learned that retained customers:

- Are less expensive to serve because they know their role in the process.

- Tend to lower marketing costs.

- Often purchase more over time.

- Are open to purchasing new and different products as they are offered.

Clearly, customers value service and whether they get good service or not, they expect it. If they don't receive service at a level that meets their expectations, they will go elsewhere until they find it. Whether the economy is on the down swing or the upswing, no one can afford to lose customers.

Many companies still deliver lousy, inept, shoddy service and even more deliver only average service.

Simply stated:	**Companies who differentiate themselves through their service have a competitive advantage.**

Why Service is Important: The Business Case

If what has been said so far doesn't convince you, let's consider building a business case for service. Let's face it, people pay more attention to something with a financial value attached to it than they do if no value or an obscure valuation is applied to it. We can understand and can account for the monetary value of items such as service charges, salaries, and stationary supplies. These numbers are easily accessible from budgets and control sheets. When we deal with a customer, we know how much of our time it will take and how much it will cost in terms of the tangible items. You may know the price of what you are selling, and you may know the actual value each transaction represents to your company. But, what about the intangibles? What are your customers really worth to your organization? And what is the pay-off to creating a Customer-Focused Organization in dollars and cents?

One of your goals in creating a customer-focused culture is to ensure that everyone understands the financial impact, good or bad, of their actions. This adds a monetary importance to each customer interaction.

Each customer represents a potential stream of income to your organization and each missed opportunity to exceed their expectations represents a reduction in potential profit.

Customer Focus 101

Here's a simple way to determine what your customers are worth. It's not totally scientific, but it sure gets the point across. We've borrowed this from a trusted colleague and mentor, Rick Tate, who borrowed it from Stu Leonard.

In the early 1990's Stu Leonard, the owner of a highly successful chain of grocery stores, came up with an interesting and simple formula for making certain every one of his employees understood the value of each customer.

He started by determining how much the average customer spent on groceries in a given week. Allowing a couple of weeks away every year for vacation, he then determined the amount an average customer spent in the course of a year. In the example

Dollars spent on groceries each week	$100.00
	x 50
Per Year	$5,000.00
Years spent in geographic area	x 10
Customer lifetime value	**$50,000.00**

shown here, he determined that the annual expenditure was $5,000.00. He was able to determine that an average customer remained in his market area for about 10 years. He multiplied these two numbers to determine the life time value of an average customer. In his case it worked out to $50,000.00.

He then made sure that all his employees understood that if they did something that caused their customers to FROWN, the financial consequences could be significant to the company that issued them their weekly paycheck. The result was profound.

A FROWN = $50,000

His employees now recognized the financial risk involved every time they interacted with a customer and acted in a way that ensured they were not knowingly responsible for losing $50,000.00.

Customer Focus 101

It is important that your employees determine what your customers are worth so that they can recognize the financial value of their actions during every customer interaction.

Here is an exercise which you can use to help you calculate what your customers are worth.

What Are Customers Really Worth?

1.1

How much is one customer worth? Take any customer segment of your business - an end user, a distributor, a private contractor. What is the annual revenue of an average customer in a particular segment?

    A. Average annual revenue $_____

    B. Revenue if they remained your customer for 5 years $_____

    C. Revenue if they remained your customer for 10 years $_____

If you lost this typical customer's business next year… what is your guess as to what percentage of that revenue loss would be profit? *(keep in mind fixed costs of the business and the fact that this business loss was not anticipated)*

    _____%

Imagine if you lost only <u>one</u> customer every day for just one year. That's 365 customers… each representing the figure above. What are the results?

365 customers X item A.   = _____ revenue loss for the year

365 customers X item B.   = _____ revenue loss over 5 years

365 customers X item C.   = _____ revenue loss over 10 years

Now Ask Yourself:

When our people are dealing with one of our customers, do they understand that they have this amount of monetary value in their hands?

When creating a business case for building a customer-focused organization, here are a few important factors to consider:

Customer Focus 101

1. It's 5 times more expensive to attract a new customer than to keep an existing one.

It is safe to say that it is far more profitable and far less costly to keep the customers you have by building their loyalty, than it is to keep replacing them with new customers.

Determining what it costs to acquire customers is a bit intangible for most people. As you can imagine, a lot goes into getting customers to walk into your place of business or call you. Advertising, merchandising, promotions, premises expense, phone systems, salaries and so on are costs associated in part with getting customers.

> If loss of 1customer = $500.00
>
> and
>
> Cost to replace one = $2,500.00
>
> What if you lost 100 customers?
>
> That's got to hurt your business!

Someone has to pay for this. Normally payment comes through the proceeds of revenue you get from the sales of your products and services. Sometimes we tend to take this for granted. Research has proven that once you have a customer, your cost of keeping him/her drops dramatically over time. When you lose a customer you will inevitably incur a higher cost to replace the one you lost.

Do you know what your defection rate is?

In other words, do you know how many customers you are losing? This formula may help you figure that out.

   a. Determine the number of customers lost in 3 months X 4 = _____

   b. Record your total number of customers = _____

   c. Express **a** and **b** as a fraction (a/b) = _____

   d. Express result of **c** as a percentage (result a/b X100 = % = Defection rate) _____

Here's an example of this calculation. Let's say you have 1000 customers. Let's further assume that in the past 3 months you have lost 50 customers. The calculations would be as follows:

   a. Customers lost $\quad\quad$ 50 X 4 = 200/year

   b. Total # Customers $\quad\quad$ 1000

   c. Fraction lost = $\quad\quad \dfrac{200}{1000} = \dfrac{1}{5}$

   d. Defection rate $\quad \dfrac{1}{5}$ X 100 = 20%

With a defection rate of 20% you would lose all your current customers over 5 years based on 20% per year.

Assuming your cost to acquire a customer is $250 and based on the fact that it is 5 times more expensive to acquire a new one, your new customer acquisition cost would be $1,250 for each new customer required to replace one that defected. Based on the example above the annual cost to replace 20% of your customer base would be $62,500. Over five years this cost would be $312,500 and you would have turned over all your customers in that period. Can you think of any better uses for the $312,500?

Customer Focus 101

2. **About 75% will do business again if the problem is resolved to their satisfaction.**
3. **95% will do business again if the problem is resolved on the spot.**

Since mistakes are guaranteed to happen, how you recover from these mistakes will significantly impact on whether the customer will do business with you again. While we will deal with this issue in greater detail in a chapter dedicated to Recovery, it is important to note that research suggests that if you recover well, your customers will stay with you. The faster you recover, if you can resolve the issue "on the spot", your customers will be impressed and in all likely-hood reward you with their continued business.

4. **Customers are willing to pay for quality service.**

In a series of polls we conducted last year with about 1000 course participants, we asked where would you prefer to spend your money? The results compare very favorably with research we have reviewed that suggests that the vast majority -70%, of customers are willing to pay for

Where would you prefer to spend your money?	
High Quality, Excellent Service, High Price	34%
High Quality, Excellent Service, Low Price	36%
Average Quality, Average Service, Average Price	2%
Low Quality, Poor Service, Low Price	15%
Non-committed	13%

high quality service. Obviously price is a variable, but service is a constant.

5. **An increase in customer loyalty will have a direct positive impact on your bottom line.**

Harvard Business Review conducted research which reveals that a 5% increase in customer loyalty can result in a return of 25% to 125% directly to the bottom line depending on your industry. It is safe to assume that investing time and resources to retain even a small number of your clients would pay for itself. You can do the math. Be conservative and take your gross profit and increase it by 25%.

6. **The cost of poor service has a direct, negative impact on your bottom line.**

Consider the time and expense associated with fixing problems, dealing with customer concerns, replacing product, re-working reports, and so on. Research from TARP (Technical Assistance Research Programs) indicates that, based on your industry, the cost can be significant.

The Cost of Poor Quality Service	
Manufacturing Industry	20% - 25% of sales revenue
Service Industry	30% - 35% of overhead costs (Source TARP)

Pick one of these two and do the calculation.

Wouldn't you like to have this as profit, rather than as an expense?

A good friend and colleague who consults with companies on creating customer focus, uses an expression which puts things into context. "People need to know the Size of the Prize." The operative word here is "prize". The financial gains associated with creating a customer-focused organization can be substantial and well worth the effort.

Customer Focus 101

Understanding Customer Expectations and Perceptions

In his book *Leadership and the Customer Revolution*, leading service and leadership expert Rick Tate suggests that we are seeing a Customer Revolution. He makes a compelling argument about how customers today find themselves in quite a different situation than in any previous economy. In the past the power was in the hands of the manufacturer or distributor and customers were usually told what they could have, when they could have it, where they could get it, how they could get it, what quality they could get and how much they would have to pay for it. And customers seemed to go along with this because that's the way it was. Goodbye Industrial Revolution…Hello Customer Revolution!

Global competition, technology and information breakthroughs, and the customer's unwillingness to be told what to expect, has resulted in the shift of power to the customer. Evidence of this power shift can be heard everywhere. You've heard it while shopping or you've exerted this power yourself. The evidence sounds like this… "Here is what I want, when I want it, where I want to get it, how I want it, the quality I desire, and how much I'm willing to pay for it. If you can't figure it out I'll go elsewhere."

Customers are better educated and have had a taste of what true extraordinary service is like from leaders in the service game. The bar has been raised as have customers' expectations, and they are willing to shop until they find someone who will meet their level of expectations. Customers vote with their feet and their wallets. That's real power.

Understanding customer expectations of the service you provided is critical. We will be covering this topic in detail in the *Learning from the Customer* Chapter. It is however very important that you understand the impact of customer expectations on your business before we go any further.

The first rule of stellar service delivery is: **Service is all about expectations**.

You buy a product; you expect it to work the first time. You go to a discount supplier, you expect the quality to be less than the high end dealer, but you still expect what you buy to work, first time every time. When it comes to products, expectations are pretty clear. People expect a good quality product based on the price they are willing to pay for it. When it comes to service, expectations can get a little fuzzy. When a customer begins a relationship with you he or she already has a specific set of expectations. These expectations are based on their perceptions of you, your company and your industry. They are formed through personal past experience, and the experience of others with whom the customer interacts.

Consider the last time you went into a self-service gas station. What did you expect? Other than the pump to be working, not much else right? After all - you are doing all the work.

You have the opportunity to Satisfy, Dissatisfy or Impress—and two of these are bad. Delivering below expectations is obviously bad, but in the context of creating loyalty, so is simply satisfying customers, because they are getting nothing more or less than they expect. Creating customer value and loyalty comes from consistently exceeding expectations.

If it exceeds your expectations, you're impressed, and

If the service you receive meets your expectations you are satisfied.

If it is below your expectations…
…well, you know.

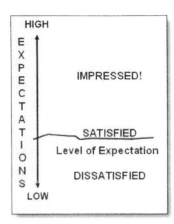

Customer Focus 101

What Do Customers Expect?

When it comes to service, what is it that customers expect? Several years ago Len Barry, a professor at Texas A& M University conducted research into what is important to customers in the context of service. This study has formed the basis for much of the work that has been done in Service Quality Improvement strategies worldwide over the last 15 years. It is as meaningful today as it was when it was first done.

Barry's research uncovered five primary dimensions to service, which impact on customers' perception of the service they have received.

These five dimensions of service are defined as follows:

Reliability Customers want services performed dependably and accurately. In other words, they want you to do what you say you are going to do when you say you are going to do it.

Responsiveness Customers want their needs met with speed and initiative. This includes accessibility to you, to information, and to others within your Company who can help when they need it. They also want you to take the initiative rather than having to ask.

Assurance Customers want service providers to be knowledgeable, courteous and trustworthy.

Empathy Customers want care and concern, and desire to be treated as an individual.

Tangibles Customers care about the tangible product or the service and the physical appearance of the facilities and people.

Of these dimension, the two of greatest importance to customers were Reliability and Responsiveness, followed closely by Assurance and Empathy. While the tangibles had some importance, this factor did not come close to the others, primarily because this is what customers were paying for.

Customer Expectations versus Customer Needs

Prof. Benjamin Schneider and Prof. David E. Bowen published an article called "Understanding Customer Delight and Outrage". Delight and outrage? That may sound a bit melodramatic but this concept is critically important to providing basic customer service. Consider this hypothetical bell curve measuring the quality of service delivery in general:

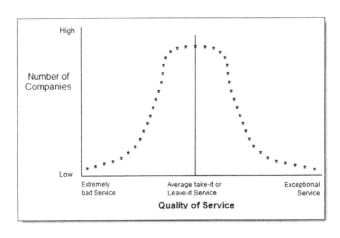

Basically, most service falls into the median of the curve - the take it or leave it level of service. If you provide this level of service the customer will be satisfied.

Customer Focus 101

You at least met their expectations. Schneider and Bowen actually break the bell curve distribution into four levels along a continuum:

Extremely bad customer service		Take it or leave it service		World class service
Outraged	Dissatisfied		Satisfied	Delighted
Defection	⟶	Ambivalence	⟶	Loyalty

Customer loyalty is the degree to which customers will patronize your business and your business alone because you've developed or created an emotional bond with them. You've gone beyond their expectations and addressed something more innate - *their emotional needs as a consumer*. Customers have come to expect fast, friendly service. They expect to get an answer to their questions. They expect you'll answer their call promptly and return their messages. Do those things well and you'll be in the game.

But will you win their loyalty? Not necessarily. If you fail, have you lost them forever? Again, not necessarily.

Research shows customers are willing to accept some failure in terms of these expectations. Fail continuously and that's a different story. This is the "ambivalence" part of the model. Next time they need your product or service they may, if it's convenient, patronize your business. But they won't seek out your business purposefully. To do that, they must be *delighted* with your service. They must be so impressed with your service that they become a dedicated follower. Schneider and Bowen refer to these customers as "apostles". They will sing the praises of your business to friends, family and coworkers.

At the other end of the spectrum it's possible to so utterly offend the basic needs of your customers that they'll willfully take every opportunity to sabotage your business. They become a terrorist according to Benjamin and Bowen. They'll tell every person who'll listen about the time your business, yada yada yada. Each time, they're likely to embellish the story.

So what creates such an extreme emotional reaction to service in some customers? According to Schneider and Bowen these reactions occur when you surpass the needs of a customer (delight) or you offend those needs. Not just fail to meet them - you (in the mind of the customer) intentionally deprived them of those needs. What are these powerful dynamics?

1. **Deprived of equity / justice**
2. **Lack of respect**

1. Deprived of equity/ justice

Customers want to be treated fairly. They want to know that the service and product they receive is as good as that received by any other customer. Consider a study done by a consumer advocate group. They asked samples of airline passengers from numerous airports what they'd paid for their ticket. They found less than 10% of passengers paid the same price for their ticket even though they flew from the same city. The results incited outrage among travelers who saw no justification for paying more, when they had received the same seating and service.

Customer Focus 101

Equity and justice is even more at issue when companies resolve customer problems. At times service or product experience is so bad customers will seek compensation for their time, effort and inconvenience. A participant in one of our customer service workshops shared the following:

"I purchased a large screen TV from one of those audio-video-electronics mega stores. The first one just did not work so we had to bring it back. The second one, which we had to wait two weeks for, had a large crack along the bottom of the screen. Again, we didn't know until we unpacked it. I'd already lost a day of work going to pick it up and unpacking it. When I brought it back they tried to charge me $37.00 because I returned it without the box. It was destroyed unpacking it. I was stunned. Even after explaining the circumstances to the retail associate he made me talk to the store manager who acted like he was doing me a favor waiving the charge."

Equity and justice means making customers feel they're getting a comparable service and product at a fair price. It also means problems are resolved to their satisfaction and that companies consider the cost of the customer's time and inconvenience when making amends.

2. Lack of respect

Nothing is more basic and elementary to effective service than the need for customers to feel respected. In fact, studies show merely respecting customers does not distinguish your business or service. That's because customers expect it. It's when they perceive a lack of respect that things get volatile.

For example:

Rachael brought her car into a repair shop to get new tires put on. After looking the vehicle over the mechanic recommended new brakes. Rachael was puzzled since she hadn't noticed any problem with the brakes. In fact, she had gotten it inspected just two months earlier. "Well they don't look 'em over the way we do." He rattled off some automotive terms to convince her. Rachael was still hesitant. "Why don't we call your husband," he said. With that Rachael told him to put the tires back on her vehicle - she'd be taking her business elsewhere.

Respect means treating customers the same - regardless of gender, race or age. It means listening to the customer's problem and responding in an empathic tone. It means your non-verbal behavior demonstrates concern and attentiveness.

Another story from a workshop participant:

"I was so sick of the service at my bank. The tellers wouldn't even acknowledge you when it was your turn in line. There was never a - Hi, how are you. They would talk over you when you were trying to explain a problem. Sometimes they would just walk away and work on something else and leave you standing there like a dope. They just always seemed like they had something more important to attend to. Eventually I took my business elsewhere."

Customer Focus 101

Perception is the Customer's Reality

Earlier we said that organizations who have achieved excellence in their service delivery share a common mind-set. A large part of this mind-set is recognizing the critical importance of customer perception.

"Perception is Reality." No doubt you have heard this expression. We hear it often. Maybe you have heard someone say, "It's only his or her perception." Unfortunately, when put in that context, people often dismiss another's perception. In reality, a customer's or anyone's perception for that matter is their reality at that moment in time. That perception can only be altered when an individual is provided with new reliable information that compels them to change their perception. Because the customer is the one in charge of whether he or she wants to do business with you, the truth is that his or her perception is the only one that matters. Right or wrong, it is his or her perception which will determine his or her actions.

Our perceptions can be strongly influenced by what we see.

Have you ever been shopping and noticed a jumbled pile of merchandise, let's say sweaters, on a table. Your initial reaction might be "What a pile of junk," even if the sweaters are expensive cashmere or "This store is disorganized" even through this sale table may have been straightened out ten minutes earlier, or "This store doesn't have enough staff, I'll never get served." On the other hand, if you saw a display of neatly folded sweaters, even if they're cheap cotton, isn't it true that you would in all likelihood initially think the merchandise is of higher quality, or the store is better organized?

A customer's perception of you or your Company is based on their past experiences with your Company, companies that offer the same products and services, and information such as stories they have heard from trusted friends, family or colleagues. If customers' past experiences have been positive, there is a good chance that their initial mind-set towards you will start off positively. If their perception is neutral or negative, quite likely that's what their mind-set will be when you approach them.

These perceptions will also influence the customer's behavior. Many people for example, always assume they will have trouble when they are purchasing a car. They expect to go through a drawn out negotiation culminating in the sales manager getting involved and offering them the "best" deal. For these people, even before they enter the showroom, they are poised for a fight or at least a spirited negotiation. Their tension levels are higher and they are not as receptive to what may be said to them because they have a preconceived notion of what is going to happen.

A deep understanding of your customers' perceptions will allow you to interact with them in a way which removes any negative perceptions and allows you to focus on what they expect, want and need.

Now that we all have a shared understanding of what service is from the customer's perspective, the financial consequences of poor service, the financial gains that can be realized through exceptional customer focus, and the significant role customer expectations and perceptions play in what motivates your customers to do business with you, we can explore what is needed to become a Customer-Focused Organization.

What is a Customer-Focused Organization?

Chapter Two

To introduce this chapter let's look at a few examples of Customer-Focused Organizations. These examples come from our own experiences or the experiences of some of the students attending our customer service training programs.

Examples of Customer-Focused Organizations

Not long ago, I signed up for an electronic account (automatic withdrawal from my savings account) with a mutual fund company. Little did I know, when setting up my account the mutual fund company had mistakenly used my checking account instead of my savings account for the electronic transfer number. Before I could catch it my personal checks were bouncing all over town. I called them in a tirade for blemishing my otherwise pristine credit. The Service Representative apologized and explained exactly what she would do to correct the mistake and when she'd call me back. What followed was amazing.

An hour later the phone rang - just as she had promised. She explained that the problem was fixed, then asked if I had moment to speak with her supervisor. Her supervisor apologized and told me that due to this error they were changing an internal procedure for verifying transit numbers. She also assured me that they were crediting my account for lost interest and penalty charges for all bounced checks. A week later I received copies of letters sent to each of my creditors explaining their mistake. The following month the supervisor called to see if there was any problem with that month's transfer.

That was five years ago. Today I have three mutual funds with that company and their service is still outstanding. Point is, they took an otherwise disastrous situation and made it one of the most memorable examples of Customer Service I've ever encountered. By doing so they won a customer.

Another example...

I bought a weedeater at Home Depot. After two months it started smoking. Assuming that wasn't normal, I took it back. Though I had lost the receipt, I was going to attempt the return anyway. I'd readied myself for battle with the frail, kindly grey-blue haired woman behind the service desk (Belle). Instead she apologized and said, "Just take one off the shelf honey. We'll send this one back." Now, I can't drive a nail in straight if my life depended on it, but just about every weekend I'm there buying something. They won a customer.

A lack of Customer Focus...

To coax our daughter into giving up her pacifier on her third birthday my wife and I offered to buy her a goldfish since she was "a big girl" now. At the pet store she saw a Lovebird and the goldfish was quickly forgotten. We got "Tiki" home, set up the cage, and introduced our new pet to the rest of the family (cat and dog). Four days later Tiki went belly up and I had to explain to a crying three year old the concept of birdie heaven. I called the pet store (large chain no doubt soon to go belly up itself) where a woman explained callously that they have a three day warranty that's only valid if you bring the bird to a vet. Industry standard

What is a Customer-Focused Organization?

she explained - "check around". We did. It was by far the worst policy of any store in our area. I started with the underpaid, un-empowered store manager, then tried to go to the district manager but couldn't get through the "Customer Service" blockade .I finally explained to the last person that would listen that I was writing the Better Business Bureau, Attorney General and calling the consumer advocate at a local TV news station. Immediately the district manager called back to fix things up. As of this writing I think they are sending a special team to the Amazon basin to snare a new Lovebird. Think about it. They wouldn't spend $39.00 to replace a Lovebird when they'd make 10 times that from a loyal customer with a bird, a dog and a cat.

You've probably heard that the U.S. has been losing its manufacturing base for some time and is becoming a "service" oriented economy. The irony is, the quality of service continues to deteriorate rapidly. Now obviously there are many companies that provide outstanding service; but, overall it's not flattering.

In the past four months this is what I have personally dealt with - no kidding:

1. Overcharged by long distance company (15 cents per minute vs. 10 cents)
2. Medical claims rejected because Insurance carrier had lost relocation paperwork
3. Shorted 4 plants from mail order garden company
4. Payment to credit card company not credited to account
5. Went to the Department of Motor Vehicles. Need I elaborate?
6. Had dinner at a franchise restaurant (Hint: It's a day of the week) I got a burger with no bottom bun and my mother-in-law found her club sandwich full of wax paper.
7. Bought some "gourmet" ice cream, Macadamia Delight. It had virtually no macadamias in it and I wasn't delighted.
8. Moved into a new house. Too many problems to list here.

These experiences really have influenced my loyalty as a consumer. My next house won't be from the same builder and my long distance service is going to be two Dixie Cups and a lot of string.

This chapter:

* provides a simple definition and description of a customer-focused organization

* provides a description of the common characteristics of a customer-focused organization

* offers an exercise to critique your own business on its customer focus

Why is this important?

Outstanding customer service can distinguish your company from your competitors. When customers walk away from your business, what will they remember? If nothing, then next time they may go to your competitor. If they remember a truly unique, satisfying experience they're more likely to return. Most companies would say "Of course we're customer-focused." But how do some earn a truly distinctive reputation compared to their peers?

What is a Customer-Focused Organization?

A Customer-Focused Organization

To get us all on the same page, here's a simple definition of a Customer-Focused Organization (CFO). A CFO is an organization:

1. whose every action is shaped by a relentless commitment to meeting and exceeding its customers' expectations regarding product and service quality,

2. who constantly evaluates and improves its internal processes to meet those expectations, and

3. whose employees are aware of their role in maintaining a valued relationship with their customers.

Let's break up that definition and see specifically how it could be translated into action. We'll use the adjacent model to do this:

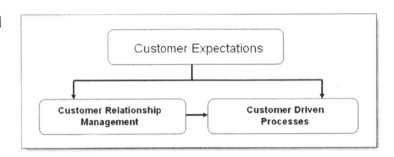

1. Customer Expectations

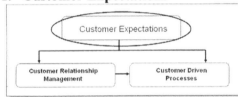

"...every action is shaped by a relentless commitment to meeting and exceeding its customers' expectations regarding product and service quality..."

In the previous chapter we talked about the critical importance of understanding your customers' expectations.

Here's an example of a relentless pursuit to identifying what customers really think about service.

John Zimbrick is the owner of a highly successful, customer-focused Honda dealership. He knew that his business was doing well. He also knew that it could do better. He kept asking customers, "What can we do to improve?" They said, "John, You're wonderful." He replied, "I know we're not that good." So John came up with a scheme to find out what customers really thought about service and how it could be improved.

John set up a system of having cab drivers take his customers to work as a value-added service after customers had dropped their cars off for service. "I got a lot of feedback that was good, but that wasn't the real benefit. The real benefit was that in a taxi cab, they'd tell people what went really well and what didn't go so well, more often than they'd tell us. They'd spill their guts on their way to work in a taxi cab. And what I started doing then was, once a quarter, I'd take my cab drivers to dinner at my country club. The cab drivers tell me and my staff what they've heard from customers. It works beautifully. And the drivers are really into it. Now a customer jumps into the cab and says, 'How's the ball game? Ball game, hell," says the driver, "How was the service?" The cabbies take notes and collect information.

What is a Customer-Focused Organization?

John has even installed a hotline so they can make immediate calls. "One time a customer told a cabbie, 'This didn't go so well.' The cabbie wrote it down. After he dropped the customer at work, he immediately called Zimbrick Honda and said, 'Hey, I got one here. Here's the name, the place. I just dropped him off. He wasn't too happy.' By the time the customer got to his office, the phone was ringing. It was someone from Zimbrick Honda asking, "I understand you're not happy. How can I help you?"

Here's an example of a relentless pursuit to meeting customers' needs. Unfortunately the company misunderstood their market and their customers' needs.

A family-owned chain of paint stores, Company P, had built its business by catering to the weekend handyman. Well known for its individualized service Company P grew a reputation as a "family helping your family." An opportunity arose to diversify the business into the wholesale market by merging with another chain. In particular, it might position them to better serve painting contractors that were turning more and more to the "mega-warehouse" type outlets for better pricing. Management at Company P thought long and hard before deciding to stick with what had made them successful. Housing starts were stagnant and the regional economy didn't seem to support an effort to expand. Besides, expansion might disrupt their culture and service directed at families. They felt safer doing what they had always done best. However, within a year the economy turned upward and demand for construction was on a steady rise.

Competitors of the small chain, who had positioned themselves to distribute to contractors, were swamped with business. Most had set up electronic ordering and billing with large painting contractors. In addition, their ability to buy paint in bulk from manufacturers meant they could pass along savings to the individual retail consumer. Before it could react, Company P lost its hold on the regional market and had to close one third of its stores to stay in business.

Company P had failed to effectively analyze the expectations of its market. Meeting the needs of wholesale contractors who had become the bulk of their potential business required a major shift in operations - an understanding of industrial products, information systems supportive of wholesale distribution, wholesale pricing structures, individualized account managers, bulk delivery services. Not only did they miss the opportunity of building a wholesale business, but they also lost retail customers because the service provided by their competition was equal to their own and their prices were cheaper. If Company P had differentiated themselves in the way they delivered their service it would have been a different story. But from the customers' perspective they were no different from their competitors except they were more expensive. Research shows that customers will pay more if the perceived value of the service provided to them meets or exceeds their expectations.

Every employee in a CFO understands that simply satisfying the customer is not enough. They recognize that customer loyalty can only be attained if they consistently endeavor to ensure that each customer's experience is memorable, in a positive way and better than what the customer would experience elsewhere. This requires that they have processes in place to continually find out what their customers want, need and expect.

What is a Customer-Focused Organization?

They have specific mechanisms in place for gathering feedback directly from customers, as well as data on industry trends such as:

- Customer Surveys

- Customer Focus Groups

- Internal Customer Service assessments

- Benchmarking information

They know that customers expect a quality product at a good value. So they focus their attention on:

1. Verifying their customers' expectations regarding quality: what the customer measures when it comes to the quality of their product, services and service

2. Identifying ways that significantly distinguish their product or service from their competitors
3. Identifying what their competitors do better in the eyes of their customers
4. identifying what they need to do internally to enhance the customer experience

Although we will be going into considerable detail about gathering customer feedback in the Know Your Customer chapter, we thought we would give you another example of a very innovative, very personal way to understand your customer's experience to illustrate this point.

At one of the mega-hardware chains, where management wanted to gather feedback from its customers, they implemented the "Roving Reporter" program. As customers entered the store a greeter would offer them a certificate worth 10% of their purchase if they took a small handheld tape recorder with them and commented on their experience as they shopped. When they paid for their goods, they could redeem their certificate and return the recorder. According to the district manager the feedback was phenomenal. The uniqueness and creativity of the program seemed to make customers more vigilant and creative.

Customers offered suggestions on:

- *how service representatives could be more proactive and approachable*

- *products lines that weren't carried that should be*

- *products that could be grouped together for more convenience*

- *ways to display pricing that made it easy for shoppers to quickly scan products*

- *creation of product kiosks that help customers via self-service*

Now let's move on to Customer Driven Processes, in other words, how CFO's deliver service based on their customers' expectations.

What is a Customer-Focused Organization?

2. Customer Driven Process

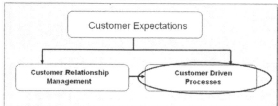

"...who constantly evaluates and improves its internal processes to meet those expectations..."

If you have ever been told "It's not our policy" or "Our system does not permit this" you'll relate to this. Even when you have great customer service staff, if your systems and procedures make it inconvenient or impossible to deliver excellent service, the system wins every time. CFO's ensure that their internal systems, processes, policies and procedures are designed to enable customer contact staff to impress their customers.

Here's an example of a customer process that, while intended to enhance service, actually did the opposite.

> *A colleague of ours explains an experience he had at a nationally-known ice cream store.*
>
> *A very friendly young woman asked, "Can I help you?" I said, "Yeah." She countered, "What flavor?" I responded, "Let me look." As I was looking, another woman behind the counter whispered something in the young woman's ear. The young woman called me back over and said, "Sir, excuse me. Before I serve you, you'll have to take a number." I said, "This intrigues me. Can I talk with the manager?" She answered, "That's her," pointing to the other woman behind the counter. I asked, "Can you explain to me why in order to get some ice cream and give you money, I have to take a number <u>when there's nobody else here</u>? I can understand the number process, but I'm confused." The manager countered, "Did she ask you to take a number?" I said, "Yes." The manager said, "That's our policy. You'll have to take one." I took a number and said, "Listen, I have a number. Is it possible for me to get an ice cream and pay you money? Have I done enough now?" The young woman answered, "Yes, sir." She looked at the digital display, looked me square in the eye and said, "21, please." I looked at my number and stood silently. She looked over her shoulder and the digital display, clicked a button and said, "Number 22." I stood silently. She repeated the process and said "Number 23?" I took pity on her as she was not the problem. I handed her my number 27 and asked, "Will this do?" She smiled hesitantly and said, "Yes, sir." She hit the number counter quickly and rattled, "23, 24, 25, 26, 27." I thought to myself, "Why are we doing this?" and said aloud, "Listen, you know what? I don't want an ice cream anymore because I don't think you really ought to treat your customers this way. I just wanted to see how far you'd go with this silly process." I started to walk out, looked at the young woman and asked, "Don't you think this is stupid?" Out of the corner of her eye, she glanced at her boss and answered, "Yeah."*

There are a significant number of organizations that create and actively administer policies that make little sense from the customer's standpoint. Procedures are important for ensuring fair and consistent service to customers; however, adherence to procedures that do not apply in a given situation can result in customer service problems. Rigidity that frustrates customers and employees usually results in higher employee turnover and apathy as well as one less customer to serve.

What is a Customer-Focused Organization?

Consider this example provided by one of our students in a service training session:

The student's healthcare company was faced with a backlog of scheduling doctor-to-doctor reviews in their Physician Review department. This review process was considered critical to monitoring the quality of service delivery to their patients. This review process resulted in the assignment of a certification number (the number of days authorized for particular clinical diagnostics for a patient). Doctors would be compensated based on this certification process and receive incentives based on the quality of care provided.

Digging a bit deeper they found an unusually high number of calls from doctors asking for an explanation of their certification. These calls were interfering with the ability of administrative staff to quickly and efficiently schedule Peer Reviews.

A report from their Customer Service System showed that many calls were specifically related to certification letters generated automatically by their computer system. By altering the language of those letters and adding greater clarification, calls regarding certification were reduced by 65%. Likewise the backlog of Physician Reviews dropped and, according to satisfaction surveys, network doctors were pleased that access to their reviews was so easy.

> **CFO's constantly look for ways to ensure their processes are better, faster and more customer-focused.**

They look for ways to improve productivity, reduce wasted time and effort and enhance their service reputation.

Action

To determine how well your company or department is aligned to meet customer needs - ask yourself these key questions:

1. How does your company quantify feedback from your customers?

2. Do you know their top 10 service complaints?

3. How would you arrange them by priority?

4. How is feedback channeled from your service department or customer service reps to management? Is it?

5. Is Customer Feedback regularly reviewed by your management?

6. How is Customer Feedback used for Business Planning and Management purposes?

7. How do you use it to identify new products and services - not just improve the process for existing ones?

What is a Customer-Focused Organization?

3. Customer Relationship Management

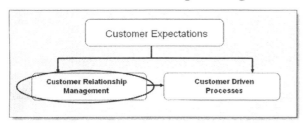

"...whose employees are aware of their role in maintaining a valued relationship with their customers."

Product and service quality aside, CFO's ensure that their employees know what they need to do to ensure that each customer feels he or she were the single most important customer every time he or she deals with them. This is the least tangible aspect of service - but one of the most important. Here's why...

Let's take a look at the hypothetical bell curve for customer service we showed you in the previous chapter.

As mentioned earlier, the quality of service overall has been on a noticeable downturn. During most interactions with businesses customers seem to be willing to accept some degree of bad service. A poor selection of fruit. A moody sales associate. A customer service person who can't solve our problem but smiles because they have been told they have to or being asked if we want "fries with that". Ironically, that's "normal." That's the "Take it or leave it" portion of the above curve.

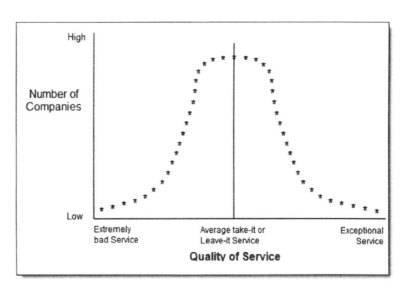

We can take it or leave it because we're neither "depressed nor impressed" when we walk away. We remember really bad service and we remember the really good service (tails of the curve). But most times we go on our way, an uncommitted customer. If those businesses had managed our interaction just a little differently we could have walked away feeling quite differently. Here's how to win over the opinions of those "Take it or leave its."

CFO's recognize that truly exceptional service can only be achieved if every employee understands that no one is more important than the customer. They ensure that all employees, regardless of their position in the company understand how their work contributes to the customer experience and what they need to do to consistently impress each customer. They recognize the value of each customer relationship and they provide employees with the knowledge and skills necessary to build and maintain strong customer relationships.

What is a Customer-Focused Organization?

Here are a few examples of what many CFO's do in order to focus their employees on enhancing customer relationships.

CFO's personalize their service

It's safe to assume that people want to be treated with respect rather than feel like a nameless, faceless John Q Public. An introduction and referring to customers by name has been shown to immediately increase trust and credibility. CFO's ensure that their staff know and practice effective Customer Service Skills and know how to place the customer at center stage. They also know that by validating a customer's anger or frustration - "I apologize for taking so long. I can understand why you're upset." - demonstrates that they are genuinely concerned with their personal satisfaction. They focus their attention on ensuring that the customer does not leave dissatisfied.

CFO's give customers more than they expected

We're not talking about the complimentary ice scraper you get at the credit union, the paint stirrer from the mega-paint store, or the 10% discount for ordering bulk from the garden mail order company. While those are nice perks, they're given to everyone. You won't walk away _feeling_ any different. Don't you notice when someone personally goes beyond your normal expectation of service to assist you? A participant in a Customer Service Skills workshop offered the following experience.

> *"I bought bricks for a patio and in casual conversation with the sales clerk I mentioned the need to put up a split rail fence in my yard. The next day the manager from the "brick store" called me at work because he knew of a reputable wholesaler who had the rails in stock at a discount. Next time I or anyone I know needs bricks - I'll think of that guy."*

CFO's seek customer and employee input and ideas

Lots of places attempt customer surveys. Some have them conveniently located at the check out counter. You'll probably get a survey in the mail after buying a car. Some businesses have cleverly arranged for telephone surveys where if you call in and provide feedback they give you a code number for discounts or free products. Surveying customers is difficult. Return rates are typically poor and you're more likely to hear from the ones that are angry. At a manufacturing company that we assisted with a Malcolm Baldrige assessment they had a very noticeable technique. Their policy - every time any person came in contact with an external customer (suppliers, retail store, parts distributor, corporate clients, etc.) the last thing they were expected to say was "Is there any way we could improve our service for you?" It was expected of *every* person. To follow up they had online databases for tracking the suggestions and feedback. Any time a suggestion was implemented a letter went to the customer signed by the staff person they dealt with and the Vice President of Quality. Effective probing is a good way to get feedback from that 80% who might otherwise "Take it or leave it."

Another company, a large appliance wholesaler, contacted former customers and offered FREE servicing for 3 months. All customers who responded in that 3 month period could get a technician to come to their house to fix one of their appliances (free service - up to $150.00 in parts). During the visit the technician asked the customer to complete a product questionnaire and

What is a Customer-Focused Organization?

also did some additional probing for feedback. The result was incredible. Of the participating customers, 86% were repeat customers (within one year bought at least one additional appliance product) and the store gathered detailed information on product preferences and how customers were using them.

CFO's recognize and reward their staff for building customer relationships and delivering exceptional service

Managers and supervisors in CFO's consistently talk about the customer in real life terms - not as an abstract concept or buzzword. For instance, the COO of Value Behavioral Health, a healthcare company, publishes a monthly newsletter on customer commitment. Each time a customer compliments a staff person (by letter or phone) the customer's comments are published along with the staff person's name. They embed outstanding service performance standards into their performance management systems. They also ensure that others involved in the service delivery chain, who may not have direct contact with customers but who assisted in the success of a service interaction, are recognized and acknowledged for their contribution.

In addition, make it your staff's responsibility to recognize the achievements of their peers. Constantly remind them to take the time to nominate others for rewards or recognition for outstanding service. Recognize outstanding customer service in your staff's performance evaluations.

One package delivery company has a "Wall of Fame." Along one wall in the main lobby is a gallery of employee photos with stories about their particular service deed and comments from customers. These are visible signs of commitment to being customer-focused.

Our consultants did some work with the service unit of a large bank who was serious about their customer relations. They had clearly defined processes for dealing with customer inquiries, angry customers and customers in need of product or service education. They trained their staff in how to handle these types of customer calls. They defined how service representatives could help callers clarify problems, offer alternatives and arrive quickly at a resolution. To ensure that ideal customer support was occurring they had a trainer who audited a sampling of calls, rated the representative on their exchange and then offered feedback on how they could improve. Their scores made up 40% of their performance evaluation.

Below is a sampling of questions from their audit instrument:

1. Representative offered a cordial greeting including name and company unit?
2. Representative assisted caller in defining and prioritizing inquiries/issues?
3. Representative accurately evaluated inquiry according to internal policies and procedures?
4. Representative maintained a professional tone if/when a customer was belligerent?
5. Representative was efficient in use of Inquiry Tracking?
6. As necessary, representative escalated inquiry to team supervisor?

What is a Customer-Focused Organization?

7. If transfer was required representative introduced caller to internal department?

8. Representative ended call with offer of appropriate follow-up and/or confirmation that customer was satisfied with service?

9. Representative documented inquiry as appropriate?

Each question was rated on a scale of 1 to 5 (unacceptable to exceptional). Each month reps got a report card on their performance. Admittedly many places use this type of call monitoring. What we found so impressive about their application was the use of real data to identify development needs and the fact that they continuously "raised the bar." Once all reps reached an average score of 4.8 or higher the manager found ways to increase their level of service. That included callbacks to verify resolution on inquiries and partnering with loan managers to survey customers on bank service.

> **Enabling employees to treat customers like unique individuals and taking actions which will at the very least satisfy each customer is the crux of Customer Relationship Management.**

Common Characteristics of Customer-Focused Organizations

What do customer-focused companies who are known for their stellar customer service have in common? We have amalgamated the results of several extensive research studies on this subject which included many of the top-rated service providers in North America. The characteristics recorded below represent the actions all these surveyed organizations indicated contributed to their success. The actions which they took which contributed to creating customer focus include:

a) Embedded a shared vision of service and defined a set of clear service values.

b) Communicated and reinforced a deep commitment to the customer among employees.

c) Recognized that every function in the company has an impact on the customer.

d) Developed and implemented support functions that taught and reinforced service behavior.

e) Defined the unique and pivotal role managers and supervisors play in reinforcing quality and service and trained them to be customer-focused leaders.

f) Recognized that Customer Satisfaction was a reflection of Employee Satisfaction. You could have perfect processes and policies but if employees weren't motivated, recognized and committed to the cause, service would suffer.

What is a Customer-Focused Organization?

g) Aligned their processes and procedures to ensure a quality customer experience.

h) Trained managers, supervisors and employees to reinforce service behaviors.

i) Defined performance standards for staff that illustrated service behavior and expectations.

j) Utilized pro-active service recovery as a means to strengthening customer relationships.

k) Provided recognition and reward for employees who exemplified stellar service.

l) Used data to measure the efficiency of internal processes.

The chapters that follow in this book will address these characteristics and provide you with suggested actions you can take in order to develop these characteristics within your Company, Organization, Department or Team.

To get you started, why not take a few minutes to complete this exercise.

Exercise

2.1

How Customer-Focused Are You?

This exercise will assist you in determining your current level of customer focus. It can be used as an initial assessment or as a discussion document for management to draft a more detailed plan for becoming more customer-oriented.

1. **Determining Customer Satisfaction**

In the spaces provided below record your answers to the following questions.

a. In terms of your products and services, what do your customers consider the most important aspects of quality? What makes your products and services the best?

_____

_____

_____

_____

_____

_____

What is a Customer-Focused Organization?

b. How have you confirmed your customers' expectations regarding service quality? How do you really know what your customers expect from your products and services?

_____

_____

_____

_____

_____

2. How do you use feedback from your customers to improve the quality of your products and services?

a. Describe the process. How is feedback gathered, reviewed, prioritized, then translated into improvement? Describe what's really happening vs. what should happen.

_____

_____

_____

_____

b. Give three (3) specific examples of how you've used customer feedback to make improvements.

_____

_____

_____

_____

3. Put yourself in the shoes of one of your customers and answer the following question:

What attitudes/behaviors do you expect of someone when you're dealing with this organization?

_____

_____

_____

What is a Customer-Focused Organization?

4. **How do you monitor, reinforce and reward those attitudes/behaviors?**

    a. What attitudes/behaviors do you expect of your staff when they deal with customers and how have you communicated them?

_____

_____

_____

_____

    b. What service attitudes/behaviors do you currently monitor and how do you reinforce or reward the desired service behavior?

_____

_____

_____

_____

5. **Right now, what are your top 5 opportunities for improvement according to your customers?**

1. _____

_____

2. _____

_____

3. _____

_____

4. _____

_____

5. _____

_____

What is a Customer-Focused Organization?

6.   List at least 3 *new* things that would distinguish your customer focus: specific initiatives/actions directed at improving customer service.

_____

_____

_____

_____

_____

_____

_____

_____

_____

_____

What is a Customer-Focused Organization?

To summarize:

1. Be sure you know what your customers expect in terms of service quality (Customer Expectations)

2. Design your company structure, reporting, job requirements, accountabilities and reinforcements so you can focus completely on customer service (Customer-Driven Processes)

3. Treat every customer as if he or she is your most important customer (Customer Relationship Management)

Creating a truly Customer-Focused Organization is among the most critical and most difficult strategies to implement. The good news is if you're able to create a truly Customer-Focused Organization you can bet you're well ahead of most competitors.

Now let's turn our attention to another essential aspect of Customer-Focused Organizations: **Developing a Shared Service Vision and Service Values**.

Creating a Shared Vision and Service Values

Chapter 3

As we discussed in the previous chapter, the first two characteristics of a CFO were:

"Embed a shared vision of service and define a set of clear service values."

"Communicate and reinforce a deep commitment to the customer among employees."

Everyone needs to know the direction your company is taking when it comes to service. The more involved they are in the process and the more clearly they understand this vision, the better chance you have of moving everyone in the same direction towards that vision.

Your service values provide you with a framework for how your employees will behave. It clearly defines what service behavior is important and most valued. Your vision and service values represent your organizational DNA - the building blocks upon which your service organization is founded.

This chapter:

- provides you with an explanation of why a shared vision is important

- suggests the steps to be followed in creating a shared vision

- provides a definition of service values

- outlines the importance of embedding service values throughout the company

- provides an example of a service values and beliefs

Why is this important?

Can you imagine what it would be like if you went to listen to an orchestra play and every member of the orchestra was playing a slightly different arrangement of the same music? While some passages might sound similar, the overall experience would likely seem fragmented, disconnected and unpleasant. Everyone needs to be not only on the same page, but also on the same note on the same page. To make effective decisions for enhancing the customer experience every employee needs a framework which will guide his or her actions. Otherwise you will just get noise.

Creating a Shared Vision and Service Values

A Shared Vision Defined

The first thing we learned in Change Management 101 was that before you can change anything, there has to be common agreement on the gap that exists between where you are today and where you want to be tomorrow. When you have a collective understanding of the strategic importance of customer focus, and a vision of service shared by everyone in your organization of where you are headed, your chances of devising and implementing an effective strategy for closing the gap are maximized. Add to this, a set of shared values, and you have the essential foundation for change. This requires:

1. an agreed upon starting point,

2. a shared commitment to a goal, and

3. a set of values to guide behavior.

This is the catalyst for creating a customer-focused organization.

In most organizations, however, what vision exists is often not a shared one. Ask a ten different individuals where the Company and/or business unit is headed and you will likely get a ten different answers. They often view the vision as something the bosses came up with and something which has little to do with their world in the trenches.

As for a shared set of values to guide behavior, while these are usually clearly stated and understood, they are frequently ignored. They are ignored because the people expected to act differently very often do not know why they are required to do things differently, how their actions make a difference, how they will be measured and held accountable, and why they should change what they are currently doing particularly if they believe what they are currently doing is the best way.

There is a tendency for some to view values as a flavor of the month and if they hold out long enough it too shall pass. For others who buy-in initially to the values, when they see others performing in a manner which is in opposition to these values, with little or no consequence, they too revert to former behavior as they see little point in putting in the extra effort.

It is essential that you create a shared vision and value system for enhancing Customer Focus to which all employees are aligned. Every employee should understand the "big picture" and how the outcomes of their efforts contribute to both departmental and organizational objectives.

Creating a Shared Vision and Service Values

Characteristics of a Shared Vision

In their book, *Leadership and the Customer Revolution*, authors Rick Tate, Gary Heil and Tom Parker identify the characteristics of a shared vision. I shall endeavor to paraphrase their explanation for you.

1. A Shared Vision Is Cumulative of Personal Visions
2. Effective Visions Are a Function of Information and Dialogue
3. Effective Visions Describe a Unique Organization
4. Creating a Shared Vision is an Ongoing Process
5. Participation is Essential
6. Ensure that the Structure is Consistent with the Type of Organization You Are Trying to Create
7. Measure Your Progress and Put the Issue on the Agenda for Periodic Review
8. Get Obsessed and Stay Obsessed

1. A Shared Vision Is Cumulative of Personal Visions

Most companies send their top management off to some off-site location for a few days to craft a well worded vision statement. They then print it up and send it to everyone requesting that everyone commit to it. While this is certainly an efficient method, usually, it is viewed by most staff as Top Management's vision. Some people commit to it, most people comply with it, and some people ignore it all together. To get employee commitment, you need buy-in. To get buy-in you typically need participation. The closer the vision is to each employee's personal vision, the more likely you will get buy-in. When employees participate in this process and their ideas and input are solicited as part of the development process, you have a greater chance of getting true commitment.

We are not suggesting that you take your entire organization to an off-site meeting. This may be completely impractical. But what is practical is to take the initial vision concept which may be crafted by the senior team, and then have each department translate that vision into terms that are relevant to each department's respective situation. By providing a venue for people to share their ideas and demonstrating that their contributions are important to the success of their department and the organization, you have a greater opportunity to create buy-in.

2. Effective Visions Are a Function of Information and Dialogue

Access to information, and the opportunity to discuss its significance, is an essential building block of an effective shared vision. In reality however, most employees don't have the information and understanding of the big picture that is needed. Even if they do have access to information, many may not have sufficient training to understand its implications. Employees also often tend to have a biased view of the information they do have. They tend to filter this information through the lens of their department, division, or functional area. Providing people with the opportunity to see the world through the eyes of others is at the heart of "sharing." Continuous debate is required to create a common sense of purpose.

Creating a Shared Vision and Service Values

Bringing people together cross-functionally to discuss how their departmental visions impact each other and how they can work together for the benefit of your customers will create the kind of meaningful dialogue that reinforces buy-in.

3. **Effective Visions Describe a Unique Organization**

People like to be part of something unique. People like to be part of something special. It is hard to commit to a cause that seems mediocre. Being one of the best is not an exciting challenge for most. People want to be the very best. They want to be proud of their organization and their own contributions. They want to make a meaningful difference.

4. **Creating a Shared Vision is an Ongoing Process**

The development of a vision statement is just the beginning of the process. As mentioned above, many organizations will create a vision statement, which is then distributed across the organization. They treat it as a done deal, an item on a checklist. Rarely do companies revisit it to determine its effectiveness, clarify its meaning or engage in any discussion after it has been completed. Like any other business strategy, your vision needs to reflect economic and social realities.

5. **Participation is Essential**

Clearly, everyone working within an Organization can't participate in the creation of a vision statement at the organizational level. But as we have described above, this general statement must be internalized by employees in the context of their roles, responsibilities and objectives. You need to give employees an opportunity to contribute, challenge, or in some other way affect the department's interpretation of the vision. Through this process employees are more likely to find a way to align themselves with the vision and actually bring it to life.

6. **Ensure that the Structure is Consistent with the Type of Organization You Are Trying to Create**

Past practices have resulted in the type of organizations we have today. Therefore, if we want to create a credible shared vision of a unique type of organization, we must ensure that present practices are in keeping with the new organization we envision. You need to be prepared to makes changes to your structures, policies and procedures and align these with your vision. If you are not prepared to do this, then your vision will be meaningless.

7. **Measure Your Progress and Put the Issue on the Agenda for Periodic Review**

If we don't track and evaluate our progress on a regular basis and hold each other accountable for making it happen, creating an organizational or departmental vision will remain a "back-burner" issue. The old saw "You can't manage what you don't measure" or "You get what you pay attention to" rings true here.

Creating a Shared Vision and Service Values

8. Get Obsessed and Stay Obsessed

We have never seen a shared vision in an organization, division or department where the leader and his or her team were not passionately involved in the effort. Obsession is contagious.

Several years ago I worked for one of the five largest banks. They were ranked 5th in terms of service in the retail sector of their business and they knew that that was just not good enough.

They created a vision of being the Number 1 financial retailer in the Country. Every branch and every department involved received extensive training in what they needed to do to accomplish this. The first component of the training was for each department to establish their own vision based on the company-wide vision. Their individual visions when connected together clearly showed that by achieving their vision they would indeed become the number 1 financial retailer.

Measures were created at the organizational level and within each department and branch so that everyone could clearly see how well they were doing in terms of achieving their vision. As circumstance changed such as shifts in the economy, operational changes, levels of employment etc., they would reevaluate how they were doing and what would be required to continue to move closer to their vision. They would challenge the vision: is it still attainable? Are they measuring the right contributing factors? Has anything changed in the work environment which prohibits employees from achieving their collective and shared vision? Regular and frequent communication was provided at all levels through newsletters, meetings and other gatherings ensuring everyone had an opportunity to dialogue about how they were doing in relation to the vision.

Everyone knew exactly what they needed to do in order to contribute to achieving the vision. Service became the mantra and the customers loved it. Processes were changed to eliminate or at least minimize any negative impact experienced by the customer. New technologies were added. Branches were redesigned to be more retail focused. Customers were asked what they wanted, and everyone listened. New products and services were added in response to customer needs.

There was no doubt that the vast majority of the 30,000 plus employees were committed to the shared vision. Interestingly enough, within four years the bank achieved its vision and was indeed rated number 1 in terms of service and retail product penetration with its customers.

To this point this bank was a text book example of a shared vision at its best.

Then changes began to occur at the senior levels of the organization. The economy began to flutter, and some divisions of the bank began to feel some negative effects of an economy in downturn. Other banks had not been dormant during this period and had their own strategies in place for enhancing their service and keeping their customers and they were becoming more customer-focused. The new senior management was under pressure to improve shareholder return on investment. Greater pressure began to emerge on sales of more products and services.

Creating a Shared Vision and Service Values

While there was a stated expectation that service levels would need to continue to improve, the actions taken by decisions-makers appeared to favor sales effort and cost control. The circumstances were changing, but the vision had not. Dialogue was replaced by directives. Commitment was replaced by compliance. An emphasis on service was replaced by aggressive sales targets and drastic consequences to those who didn't achieve their targets.

The bank fell back to its original standing of number 5 in a fraction of the time it took to get to Number 1.

While the end of this story is not a happy one, it certainly does reinforce the value of creating a truly shared vision and sticking with it.

Service Values

Customer-focused organizations are built on a foundation of shared service values.

In 1914, before he hired the company's first employee, Tom Watson, Sr. of IBM, wrote:

> **"One, the individual must be respected. Two, the customer must be given the best possible service. Three, excellence and superior performance must be pursued."**

He wanted his employees to understand the kind of company he intended to build. He wanted them to know that if they demonstrated a set of values incompatible with his, they would be fired! His son, and other leaders who followed at IBM, believe that their success was built on these values.

As individuals we all have our own set of values and beliefs. Whether it's honesty, reliability, truthfulness and so on, these values and beliefs guide our actions. Service values provide your employees with the means to understand what you value when it comes to how they perform their jobs. It is essential that each employee internalizes these values and makes them their own.

Values and beliefs should be:

- Clearly articulated to everyone.
- Understood by all.
- Reinforced through accountability.

> **"Most successful customer service companies have a written, well communicated set of values which humanize the work environment by setting a tone for the way people in the organization do business. In these businesses, the values become as much a part of the company's operation as its product, service or policies."**
>
> **–Buck Rogers**

For a company's values to be considered important by its employees, they must be:

- Repeatedly communicated at meetings, training sessions and conferences.
- An integral part of the company's recruitment, training, promotion and performance appraisal systems.
- Practiced, not merely theorized, by management.

Creating a Shared Vision and Service Values

Here is a sample of the customer values at Mindspring, the Internet Service Provider who won a J.D. Power and Associates award a few years ago for best customer service in their industry.

ATLANTA (Sept. 14, 1999) Leading national Internet Service Provider, MindSpring Enterprises, Inc. received the highest ranking in overall customer satisfaction among Internet Service Providers in an independent study conducted by J.D. Power and Associates. The J.D. Power and Associates 1999 National ISP Online Residential Customer Satisfaction Study shows MindSpring's dedication to customer satisfaction, which MindSpring believes is reflected in the company's new advertising campaign tagline, "You'd be happier using MindSpring."

"We could not be more pleased by this award," said MindSpring Founder and CEO Charles Brewer. "I'm extremely proud of all of our 1,800 employees, who because of their dedication to top quality service, have allowed us to make our more than one million customers very happy."

This is the first year MindSpring has been included in the J.D. Power and Associates National ISP Online Residential Customer Satisfaction Study. MindSpring entered at the No. 1 spot with a significant lead in customer satisfaction over the other six national ISPs in the 1999 Study. More than 50 percent of U.S. residential ISP subscribers are represented by the top seven ISPs included in the Study. More than 3,400 households nationwide responded to the J.D. Power and Associates Survey and evaluated their individual ISP. Based on their responses, seven factors that determine overall customer satisfaction were identified. MindSpring received the highest marks in all categories:

- *Cost/billing/image*
- *Speed and availability*
- *Ease of Use*
- *Suitability of Services/Content*
- *Customer Care/Technical Support*
- *E-Mail Services*
- *Navigation/Access to Other Portals*

One of MindSpring's Core Values and Beliefs reads, 'We feel a sense of urgency on any matters related to our customers. We own problems and we are responsive. We are customer-driven,'" said Mike McQuary, MindSpring's president. "Our call center teams answer nearly 600,000 phone calls and send over 50,000 support e-mails each month. They do a terrific job serving the needs of our customers and it's great to be recognized for this."

Creating a Shared Vision and Service Values

Mindspring Core Value and Beliefs

✓ We respect the individual, and believe that individuals who are treated with respect and given responsibility respond by giving their best.

✓ We require complete honesty and integrity in everything we do.

✓ We make commitments with care, and then live up to them. In all things, we do what we say we are going to do.

✓ Work is an important part of life, and it should be fun. Being a good business person does not mean being stuffy and boring.

✓ We are frugal. We guard and conserve the company's resources with at least the same vigilance that we would use to guard and conserve our own personal resources.

✓ We insist on giving our best effort in everything we undertake. Furthermore, we see a huge difference between "good mistakes" (best effort, bad result) and "bad mistakes" (sloppiness or lack of effort).

✓ Clarity in understanding our mission, our goals, and what we expect from each other is critical to our success.

✓ We are believers in the Golden Rule. In all our dealings we will strive to be friendly and courteous, as well as fair and compassionate.

✓ We feel a sense of urgency on any matters related to our customers. We own problems and we are always responsive. We are customer driven.

Notice that these values are in terms every employee can relate to. They speak to behaviors that the customer can see and experience.

You will also notice that there is a direct correlation between these values and Len Barry's research in terms of what customers want and expect when it comes to service as described in Chapter 1. Here they are again, so you don't need to flip back to those pages.

Creating a Shared Vision and Service Values

These five dimensions of service are defined as follows:

Reliability — Customers want services performed dependably and accurately. In other words, they want you to do what you say you are going to do when you say you are going to do it.

Responsiveness — Customers want their needs met with speed and initiative. This includes accessibility to you, to information, and to others within your Company who can help when they need it. They also want you to take the initiative rather than having to ask.

Assurance — Customers want service providers to be knowledgeable, courteous and trustworthy.

Empathy — Customers want care and concern, and desire to be treated as an individual.

Tangibles — Customers care about the tangible product or the service and the physical appearance of the facilities and people.

When you begin to develop your own set of service values, we highly recommend that you incorporate these five dimensions of service. Then, involve your employees in discussing what they will need to do in order to perform their jobs in a manner which demonstrates these values every day. Train them and recognize and reward them when they act in accordance with these values. Hold everyone accountable every day for putting your values into action.

That will move you another step closer to creating the customer-focused organization you want.

Creating a Shared Vision and Service Values

ACTING ON YOUR SERVICE VALUES

3.1

You are the greatest ambassador of the values you establish. In fact, what you do does more to reinforce what you value than what you say.

Here's a quick checklist to see the extent to which what you value is truly customer-focused.

Please indicate whether you agree or disagree with the action taken in each situation by placing a checkmark in the appropriate column.

Situation and Action taken	Agree	Disagree
1. As a result of serving a customer, an employee misses a meeting. **ACTION:** You remind the employee that meetings are important and mandatory.		
2. You notice an employee relaxing on the job after working long hours to serve your customers. **ACTION:** You find some additional work to keep the employee occupied.		
3. A manager has produced under budget. **ACTION:** You acknowledge the effort and make a note to reduce next year's budget.		
4. An employee is hard working and loyal but does not relate well to customers. **ACTION:** You put up with it because you need the volume of work the employee produces.		
5. A manager gets results, yet does not treat employees with respect and dignity. **ACTION:** You put up with this because the department runs so efficiently.		
6. An employee appears to work hard and be busy yet his accomplishments seem vague. **ACTION:** You tell the employee to work smarter not harder.		
7. You receive complaints from employees about a manager's leadership style. **ACTION:** You tell them that they need to discuss this with their manager.		

If you agreed with any of the actions taken here, you may want to assess what you truly value. Many of you may also think that the actions taken here are improper and extreme. You would be right. The question is, what would you do? And would these actions truly reinforce the customer-focused culture you envision?

The answers to these questions are a great indicator of whether you practice a customer service mind-set and whether you are behaving in accordance with your values.

Now That's Customer Focus!

As you work through the following chapters of this book you may want to revisit these situations and based on what you learned, determine how you need to react.

Service Comes From Within

Chapter 4

Characteristics of Successful Customer-Focused Organizations:

"Recognized that every function in a company has an impact on the customer."

"Developed and implemented support functions that taught and reinforced service behavior."

In truly Customer-Focused Organizations there is a shared and unwavering belief that No One is more important than the Customer. It is also believed that the delivery of exceptional customer service and exceeding customers' expectations is not the sole responsibility of those who come into contact with customers; it's everyone's responsibility. While the customer contact person is directly involved in the customer interaction, satisfying the customer or hopefully exceeding the customer's expectations, can only happen if everyone within the Company or Organization performs their job in a way which also focuses on the customer. Regardless of the job an employee performs, those in customer contact positions rely upon them, to provide them with the tools, information or support they need to win with the customer. Employees who perform a technical function need to ensure that the technical processes and systems, for which they are responsible, function in a way which enables the customer contact employees to succeed with the customer. Those who perform an administration role need to ensure that the processes they manage are accurate and complete.

Everyone must understand how their work makes a difference to the external customer. They must respond to their co-workers with the same sense of urgency that is required of them to exceed the external customer's expectations. There must be a radical improvement in lateral communications among employees of different departments.

This chapter:

- explains how and why customer service and customer satisfaction require cooperation and partnership among employees of different functions and departments

- helps you to identify your internal service partners

- helps you assess to what degree you are a help or a hindrance to your partners and identify areas for service improvement

- discusses those situations in which people indirectly affect the value customers receive

- provides a service checklist that will allow you to see the relationship between your job and the customer's satisfaction

- helps you to identify ways to help others in the organization to provide service more effectively

Why is this important?

If you can't get things right internally, you will never get things right for the paying customer. The vast majority of service problems are caused by a breakdown within your company.

Service Comes From Within

Service Partnerships ...Internal Cooperation

Our service workshops are a great place to gather examples of just about every type of service horror story and victory. Here is a story one of our students related which illustrates the need for strong internal partnerships.

Peter works with an investment firm as a Customer Service Representative. He spends most of his time solving customer problems and providing information. He also takes calls from Financial Regulators and Agencies who sell this company's investment products. He's been with the Company for several years and can handle most of the problems he encounters. Here is a chronology of events.

10:23 AM   Peter receives a call from one of his biggest producing Agency clients who needs to get information on a major change to one of their products that has just been initiated by the Company. (Turns out that Peter must have missed the memo about this product change because he knew nothing about it.)

10:26 AM   He quickly turns to his colleague in the next cubicle. His colleague indicates he knows nothing about the change either.

10:27 AM   Peter explains to the caller that he needs to get some updated information in order to answer his questions. The caller indicates that he has one of his best customers with him and needs the answers as soon as possible. Peter asks the caller if he wants to hold or if it would be alright if he calls him back in ten minutes. The caller indicates he would rather hold since this is very important. Peter promises to get back to him as quickly as he can.

10:29 AM   Peter immediately calls his supervisor. She knows nothing about this change.

10:30 AM   Since most product changes are handled by their Product Development Department in the Marketing Division, Peter calls them. Peter explains the situation. The person he speaks with indicates he is not aware of any changes. Peter explains again that he has an important customer on the line and asks this person if he could check around. The person replies, "It's not my job. Why don't you call my supervisor."

10:35 AM   Peter calls the supervisor. Turns out he is on vacation.

10:36 AM   Peter checks back with the caller, to let him know what's happening. The caller is not impressed and takes it out on Peter. Peter apologizes for the delay and assures him that he will get the information and call him back as soon as he can. The client's response is "I'd rather wait and you better make it fast!"

10:40 AM   Peter decides to call the Finance Department since the product change has to do with the way fees and disbursements are calculated. The first person he talks to doesn't know what to suggest, since she is only responsible for reporting to regulators. She does however suggest Peter talk to Bill.

10:45 AM   Peter calls Bill who seems to know all about the changes. Bill's response to Peter is, "We sent an email to everyone last week about this. Didn't you get the email?" Peter indicates no one in his area received the email and that he has an important and very upset customer on the phone who needs answers right away. Peter asks Bill if he would join in on the call to answer the customer's questions since he seems to know all about the changes. Bill indicates that he would not be comfortable doing that and that it's contrary to company policy. In other words "It's not my job". He does however offer to send a copy of the email to Peter right away.

Service Comes From Within

10:50 AM   *Peter receives an email with a 27 page attachment. He immediately connects with the client, who has been on hold all this time, to answer his questions even though he has not had time to read the email. THE CLIENT IS GONE.*

Mutual cooperation among employees from different functions and departments is essential if your goal is to deliver superior value your customers. When it comes to customer service there is no place for an "It's not my job" attitude. Customer service must be viewed as everyone's job… everyone's most important job. The simple reality is… without the customer there is no job!

The only way to succeed is for everyone to believe that his or her job is not a series of tasks and duties, but rather an integral part of creating value for customers. Everyone should know the negative impact they have on customers when they fail to provide help or assist co-workers in the company.

You are partners… equals… with an obligation to do your best to take care of the company's customers.

With a common focus on what is vital to the company's success… your customers… you can overcome the common problems that besiege other companies.

There is absolutely no possibility of excellent customer service without excellent internal cooperation.

Allan works in the finance department of a financial services company. One of the Company's wealthy clients was questioning the accounting of several large investment transactions. Allan had previously worked in the Call Center and had worked with this particular client in the past. The Company's Call Center Customer Service Representative who initially took the client's call was uncertain about explaining the series of complicated transactions and charges that were processed through the client's accounts.

The client was getting frustrated and asked the Service Rep if he could speak with Allan. While this practice was frowned upon by the Company, the Rep knew this was the best thing to do particularly as he knew Allan would ensure that the client was provided with the correct information. Allan was more than willing to assist even though he knew this particular client was very demanding.

The Rep explained the situation to Allan and Allan began to ask the client a few clarifying questions. This seemed to irritate the client a bit more but the client was willing to go through this process as long as it meant "fixing his accounts". A few minutes into the call, Allan's boss approached his desk and began hovering around it signaling that he wanted to talk to Allan. Allan politely excused himself from the conversation with the client and indicated to his boss that he was dealing with a client. His boss told him that was not his job and then asked for a report Allan was working on. Allan told his boss he needed about 10 minutes to finish off the report. His boss told him he needed the report immediately. Allan asked "what about the client?" His boss told him to tell the client he (Allan) would get back to him within the hour.

Service Comes From Within

Allan tried to explain that this was a very important client. His boss sternly indicated to Allan that this was a very important report and that he needed it immediately.

Allan really liked his job and had worked long and hard to get it. He told the client he would get back to him within the hour. Needless to say, the client was not impressed.

Allan finished the report and took it into his boss's office. His boss told him to put the report in his in basket. He had to go to an appointment and would review it when he got back before the end of the day.

You're probably wondering what happened to the client? He took his $12 Million in investments and went to the competition.

Every day employees are faced with choosing between two or more "things" to do. When the choice involves doing something for a customer, versus doing something for the boss or co-worker, or performing some sort of internal function (such as filing, inventory, closing out a register or finishing a report), many times the customer gets "put off."

When internal cooperation and support isn't present, the person who ultimately must face the customer is left embarrassed, at best. More often the employee must take the "flack" from the customer as a result of dissatisfaction. In fact, there is nothing more stressful or frustrating to people who are responsible for the delivery of service to the customer, than to try to give outstanding service without any help from co-workers or people in other departments.

As a manager, your partners include everyone who relies on you for the work you do, including your employees.

Why not take a minute to complete the short self-assessment contained on the next page.

Service Comes From Within

Take a moment to rate yourself in the following areas. Be honest, no one is looking at the results.

1 = Never   2 = Seldom   3 = Sometimes   4 = Often   5 = Very Often   6 = Always

My Employees would say that ...	1	2	3	4	5	6
1. I am helpful and cooperative.						
2. I remove obstacles which prevent them for delivering excellent service.						
3. I am available when they need help.						
4. I am responsive and reliable.						
5. I am concerned and caring.						
6. I am empathetic to their issues.						
7. I reinforce that serving the customer is the priority.						
8. I take action quickly to correct inconvenient policies and procedures.						

If you rated yourself anything less than a 6 in every category, what do you need to do to become a six?

How do you think your employees would respond if you were to ask them to rate you?

Would they rate you the same or differently?

How do you know?

How do you think your other internal partners would respond if you were to ask them to rate you? What would they say about the rest of your work group?

These are some pretty tough questions. But in the context of creating a strong internal service foundation, the tough questions need to be addressed and acted upon.

Service Comes From Within

Characteristics of Successful Internal Partnerships

Successful Internal Service Partnerships have a number of common characteristics. These include:

1. Work product requirements are clearly understood

2. Requirements–including timeframes–are negotiated taking into consideration the needs of both partners

3. Problems are identified quickly and addressed jointly

4. Communication is two-way and free-flowing

5. Information is shared frequently

6. The quality of the partnership is linked to the quality of customer service externally

7. Work processes are well-designed and efficient

8. There is mutual agreement and commitment to actions

9. Appreciation is shown for efforts

10. Mutual respect is evident

11. Each person's contributions are valued and acknowledged

Organizations with successful internal partnerships recognize that it takes teamwork. Those who need to rely on others within their organization to help them keep their promises-whether it is shipping for delivery of orders, accounts receivables for processing accounts or any other department who is part of the process-make certain they know what is needed and they make sure they can do what is needed. They don't expect their internal partners to drop everything because they recognize that their partners may very well be getting demands on their time from others within their company. That doesn't mean they don't agree that customers are important, but there is a good chance that they have a lot on their plates and other priorities as well. Recognizing this, they take the time to work out in advance how they can work together to ensure the highest level of service.

In these organizations, all employees pride themselves as much for the service they provide, as they do for their technical expertise. They might prepare the most accurate reports, or they may be the best computer system specialist that money can buy. However, they know that if they are late in responding, or if what they provide does not fulfill their internal partner's requirements, they are failing in their obligation to their customers.

It is extremely important that every employee understands why he or she performs his or her tasks and functions. What the result is of what they do. What the outcomes are. Employees must clearly understand the contribution they make to the external customer's experience in order to see what impact they have on the retention of those customers. The job of a file clerk is not filing...it is ensuring easy retrieval of information for internal partners or external customers!

Service Comes From Within

How to Build and Strengthen Internal Partnerships

Like any business process, managing, maintaining and strengthening internal partnerships should be embedded into your on-going management practices. This requires identification, performance assessment, gap analysis, planning for improvement and on-going performance evaluation.

Action To build and maintain strong internal partnerships you need to take the following steps and answer the following questions.

Step	Questions to Consider
1. Identify your internal service partners (people or departments)	• Look at this from both viewpoints: who relies on you, and upon whom do you rely?
2. Clarify requirements	• What specifically is needed? What timeframes are part of the requirement?
3. Understand the consequences of not meeting requirements	• Communicate not only what the requirements are, but also why they are needed; what impact will it have on the external customer if the requirement is not met?
4. Assess the current quality of your Internal Service Partnerships	• How good a service partner are you? • How well are your partners meeting your requirements? • What gaps exist?
5. Identify actions to maintain your successful partnerships	Partnerships which are working well should be maintained. Without constant attention, these relationships could be in jeopardy. • Do they know they are doing well? • Do you acknowledge their contribution? • Do you give them positive feedback? • Do you meet regularly and discuss how you can continue to work well together? • Do you discuss changes in customer requirements in a timely fashion?
6. Identify actions to strengthen partnerships which need improvement	• Do you need to clarify requirements? • Do you need to negotiate or renegotiate requirements or timeframes? • Should you meet to conduct joint problem-solving? • Should you change the way you have been communicating? • Do you need to share information? • Should you define the consequences to customers of the quality of your partnership? • Does the work process you are following need to be improved? • Should you discuss and commit to mutually agreed upon actions? • Can you communicate an appreciation of their efforts? • Can you demonstrate respect and acknowledge their contributions?

Service Comes From Within

The following exercise will help you to identify your internal partners and answer many of the questions posed above. We highly recommend that you complete this exercise and then do it with all of your team.

Exercise

Who Are Your Internal Partners?

4.1

1. Fill in the boxes with the names of people or departments which you or your department need in order to serve your customers.

2. For each person or department you have listed, check either Yes or No in the tick boxes, for the two questions in the columns to the left.

3. For each person or department, rate how well they are currently doing in meeting your needs. Circle your rating of 1 (poor) through 6 (excellent).

On a scale of 1 to 6, how well are they doing?	Do they understand the consequences to my customers?		Do they understand my requirements		Who are the Internal Service Partners that you/your department need in order to serve your customers?	
	YES	NO	YES	NO	**People or Department**	
1 2 3 4 5 6	☐	☐	☐	☐		Y o u — Y o u r
1 2 3 4 5 6	☐	☐	☐	☐		
1 2 3 4 5 6	☐	☐	☐	☐		
1 2 3 4 5 6	☐	☐	☐	☐		
1 2 3 4 5 6	☐	☐	☐	☐		
1 2 3 4 5 6	☐	☐	☐	☐		
1 2 3 4 5 6	☐	☐	☐	☐		
1 2 3 4 5 6	☐	☐	☐	☐		
1 2 3 4 5 6	☐	☐	☐	☐		

Service Comes From Within

Who Are Your Internal Partners?

4.1

1. Fill in the boxes with the names of people or departments which need you or your department in order to serve their customers.

2. For each person or department you have listed, check either Yes or No in the tick boxes, for the two questions in the columns to the right.

3. For each person or department, rate how well you believe you/your department is currently doing in meeting their needs. Circle your rating of 1 (poor) through 6 (excellent).

	Who are the Internal Service Partners that need you/your department in order to serve their customers	Do I understand their requirements?		Do I understand the consequences to their customers		On a scale of 1 to 6, how am I doing?
	People or Department	YES	NO	YES	NO	
D E P A R T M E N T		YES ☐	NO ☐	YES ☐	NO ☐	1 2 3 4 5 6
		YES ☐	NO ☐	YES ☐	NO ☐	1 2 3 4 5 6
		YES ☐	NO ☐	YES ☐	NO ☐	1 2 3 4 5 6
		YES ☐	NO ☐	YES ☐	NO ☐	1 2 3 4 5 6
		YES ☐	NO ☐	YES ☐	NO ☐	1 2 3 4 5 6
		YES ☐	NO ☐	YES ☐	NO ☐	1 2 3 4 5 6
		YES ☐	NO ☐	YES ☐	NO ☐	1 2 3 4 5 6
		YES ☐	NO ☐	YES ☐	NO ☐	1 2 3 4 5 6
		YES ☐	NO ☐	YES ☐	NO ☐	1 2 3 4 5 6

Service Comes From Within

Maintaining Internal Partnerships

Partnerships which are now working well should be maintained. Without constant attention, these relationships could be in jeopardy.

This activity will focus your attention on those partnerships which are currently strong and allow you to identify things which you can do to ensure that they stay that way.

1. In the space below, write the names of the people or departments you listed in the previous exercise for which you answered "yes" to both questions **and also** circled a rating of 5 or 6.

_____

_____

_____

_____

_____

_____

2. Select a maximum of three of the partners from question #1 and complete the following checklists.

#1: Internal partner _____

Question	Yes	No
Do they know they are doing well?	☐	☐
Do we acknowledge their contribution?	☐	☐
Do we give them positive feedback?	☐	☐
Do we meet regularly and discuss how we can continue to work well together?	☐	☐
Do we discuss changes in customer requirements in a timely fashion?	☐	☐

What else can you do to maintain this partnership?

_____

_____

_____

_____

Service Comes From Within

#2: Internal partner _____

Question	Yes	No
Do they know they are doing well?	☐	☐
Do we acknowledge their contribution?	☐	☐
Do we give them positive feedback?	☐	☐
Do we meet regularly and discuss how we can continue to work well together?	☐	☐
Do we discuss changes in customer requirements in a timely fashion?	☐	☐

What else can you do to maintain this partnership?

_____

_____

_____

_____

#3: Internal partner _____

Question	Yes	No
Do they know they are doing well?	☐	☐
Do we acknowledge their contribution?	☐	☐
Do we give them positive feedback?	☐	☐
Do we meet regularly and discuss how we can continue to work well together?	☐	☐
Do we discuss changes in customer requirements in a timely fashion?	☐	☐

What else can you do to maintain this partnership?

_____

_____

_____

_____

You may wish to continue this activity with other internal partners you have identified.

Service Comes From Within

Strengthening Internal Partnerships

4.3

This activity will focus your attention on those partnerships which are not currently strong and allow you to identify things which you can do to strengthen these relationships.

1. In the space below, write the names of the people or departments you listed in Who Are Your Internal Partners exercise which you did not transfer to the Maintaining Internal Partnerships exercise 4.2.

_____

_____

_____

_____

2. Select a maximum of three of the partners from question #1 and complete the following checklists.

#1: Internal partner _____

Question	Yes	No
Do we need to clarify requirements?	☐	☐
Do we need to negotiate or renegotiate requirements or timeframes?	☐	☐
Should we meet to conduct joint problem-solving?	☐	☐
Should we change the way we have been communicating?	☐	☐
Do we need to share information?	☐	☐
Should we define the consequences to customers of the quality of our partnership?	☐	☐
Does the work process we are following need to be improved?	☐	☐
Should we discuss and commit to mutually agreed upon actions?	☐	☐
Can we communicate our appreciation of their efforts?	☐	☐
Can we demonstrate respect and acknowledge their contributions?	☐	☐

What else can you do to strengthen this partnership?

_____

_____

_____

Service Comes From Within

#2: Internal partner _____

Question	Yes	No
Do we need to clarify requirements?	☐	☐
Do we need to negotiate or renegotiate requirements or timeframes?	☐	☐
Should we meet to conduct joint problem-solving?	☐	☐
Should we change the way we have been communicating?	☐	☐
Do we need to share information?	☐	☐
Should we define the consequences to customers of the quality of our partnership?	☐	☐
Does the work process we are following need to be improved?	☐	☐
Should we discuss and commit to mutually agreed upon actions?	☐	☐
Can we communicate our appreciation of their efforts?	☐	☐
Can we demonstrate respect and acknowledge their contributions?	☐	☐

What else can you do to strengthen this partnership?

_____

_____

_____

_____

Service Comes From Within

#3: Internal partner _____

Question	Yes	No
Do we need to clarify requirements?	☐	☐
Do we need to negotiate or renegotiate requirements or timeframes?	☐	☐
Should we meet to conduct joint problem-solving?	☐	☐
Should we change the way we have been communicating?	☐	☐
Do we need to share information?	☐	☐
Should we define the consequences to customers of the quality of our partnership?	☐	☐
Does the work process we are following need to be improved?	☐	☐
Should we discuss and commit to mutually agreed upon actions?	☐	☐
Can we communicate our appreciation of their efforts?	☐	☐
Can we demonstrate respect and acknowledge their contributions?	☐	☐

What else can you do to strengthen this partnership?

_____

_____

_____

_____

Service Comes From Within

Who is Responsible for Service?

The answer to this question is simple. Everyone, right? Well, yes and no. Everyone in your organization must be accountable for the delivery of exceptional service, of that there is no doubt.

But…

If I were to ask you who was responsible for sales in your company you would probably give me the name of the person in charge of sales and marketing.

If I were to ask you who is responsible for financial matters you would probably give me the name of your controller, head of finance or some such person.

If I were to ask you who is responsible for computer systems you would probably give me the name of the head of your IT Department.

When I ask this question in training sessions with management, "Who is responsible for Service?" the typical response I get is the name of the person in charge of a call center or customer service or nothing at all. Rarely do I get the name of an executive level person responsible for driving a customer-focused strategy.

I could go on, but I think you get the point. Now, some of you who run smaller companies may wear multiple hats and I acknowledge that, but don't you think it's interesting that when it comes to something as strategically important as service and creating customer focus across your entire organization, there is a high probability that no one is ultimately responsible for turning your customer-focused strategy into action, for ensuring that training is done, for removing obstacles to effective service delivery, for developing supporting measurements for ensuring you stay on track and continue moving towards your vision?

The research results we showed you in Chapter Two revealed that the top customer-focused companies take this seriously and put experienced people into place to lead the customer-focused charge and make things happen.

Service Comes From Within

You do have a couple of options. You can create a department headed by customer focus specialists who have the authority to make things happen, or you can form a senior team, sometimes referred to as a Customer Focus Steering Committee, who takes on the role of driving the strategy. Each has its advantages and disadvantages but the key here is to empower whomever is driving the transition to a customer-focused culture with the means to make things happen.

Enough said. The next step is up to you.

Now that you are building a solid foundation based on strong internal service and cooperation you are ready to focus on the next issue: Customer-Focused Leadership.

"Things that matter most must never be at the mercy of things that matter least"

Customer-Focused Leadership

Chapter 5

Characteristics of Successful Customer-Focused Organizations:

"Defined the unique and pivotal role managers and supervisors play in reinforcing quality and service and trained them to be customer-focused leaders."

"Recognized that Customer Satisfaction was a reflection of Employee Satisfaction. You could have perfect processes and policies but if employees weren't motivated, recognized and committed to the cause, service would suffer."

If your goal is to create a customer-centric culture throughout your company then you will need to embed service into everything you do.

While service is everyone's responsibility, this is particularly true for anyone who manages and supervises others. That's why we believe that...

... service is a Leadership issue.

To become a service leader, it is helpful to look at the best practices of other organizations when it comes to management and leadership practices and tailor these to your specific situation.

In this chapter we will explore key customer-focused leadership principles so that you can determine how these can be applied within your organization.

This chapter:

- explains why service is a leadership issue

- defines ten key Customer-Focused Leadership Principles (Best Practices)

- provides you with a method to assess your current level of customer-focused leadership

Why is this important?

Truly customer-focused organizations are run and managed on a day-to-day basis by Customer-Focused Leaders. The buck stops with you.

NOTE: At the end of this chapter we have provided a simple form that you can copy and use to jot down your thoughts based on questions that we will be posing throughout this chapter.

Customer-Focused Leadership

Service is a Leadership Issue

Customer-contact and support employees are rarely the biggest obstacle to service improvement.

It's up to management to create an environment in which employees can deliver excellent service.

The reality is that you can talk about how important service is from the highest levels of your company, you can begin to change processes and procedures company-wide which reinforce customer-focus, and your staff can work diligently at trying to provide service excellence. But, at the end of the day, the only way to ensure sustainable service excellence is for those in management positions throughout your company to do things which create an environment where service flourishes. You will make it happen.

Your Key Role as Leaders:

- To build and maintain the conditions that make service excellence possible and worthwhile

- To make it real operationally

- To make it stick culturally

> ...in other words, to be a Customer-Focused Leader.

Organizations that deliver top quality service have a number of things in common. These best practices have been summarized into ten key customer-focused leadership principles.

These are:

I.	**Commit to Service Excellence**
II.	**Be Pro-Active in Recovery**
III.	**Enhance and Align your Systems**
IV.	**Listen to the Voice of the Customer**
V.	**Lead with a Customer Focus**
VI.	**Define Service Boundaries**
VII.	**Provide Autonomy**
VIII.	**Measure What's Important**
IX.	**Accountability for All**
X.	**Recognize and Reward**

Let's take a look at each of these in more detail.

Customer-Focused Leadership

Best Practices in Customer-Focused Leadership

1. Commit to Service Excellence

Most managers and staff typically say that service is important. The question is, do they act consistently in a way which demonstrates that service is important? A true commitment to service is based on the belief that service excellence is a competitive advantage. The term commitment in this principle means action. It is what you do as leaders, not what you say that counts. The best evidence of your commitment is found in what customers and your internal service partners say about you and your team.

| Action |

Ask yourself the following questions. Jot down what you need to do differently, based on your answers.

1. What do the people who report to me consider to be the most important aspect of their job?
2. In the last two weeks, what actions have I taken which demonstrate my commitment to Service Quality?
3. What can I do to ensure that our customers and/or internal service partners tell positive stories about the way we treat them?

2. Be Pro-Active in Recovery

Recovery is a term which describes your actions in response to a customer's complaint or problem. Even with a goal of "zero defects," people make mistakes. It is important to remember that the vast majority of customers don't complain about the quality of the service they receive, they just leave. Problems will happen and should be viewed as opportunities to impress the customer and create positive stories.

In the world of service recovery, the faster the problem is resolved the more likely the customer will be satisfied. Work with your staff to ensure that the solutions provided to customers are designed to at the very least satisfy, but whenever possible impress.

Since the most frequent complaints and problems are predictable, you can work with your staff to plan recovery strategies for handling these complaint situations and empower your staff to take action.

Being pro-active also means seeking out disgruntled customers before they have a chance to complain, particularly when you know that as a result of a change in a process or procedure, complaints are likely to result. It's about building solid relationships with each customer based on trust, honesty and a sincere desire to earn their loyalty.

| Action |

Ask yourself the following questions. Jot down what you need to do differently, based on your answers.

1. Have I as a leader communicated to my people the importance of effective recovery processes?
2. How have I empowered my people to take action in recovery situations?

Customer-Focused Leadership

3. How have I helped my people predict potential problems and build plans for addressing these in a way which impresses our customers?

4. What communication pipeline have I created to ensure that our customers and/or internal service partners tell us their concerns?

3. Enhance and Align your Systems

An organization's survival depends upon rapid, continuous enhancement to all processes, policies and systems which impact on the customer. Many processes are designed to meet regulatory, compliance and fiduciary standards. Other processes have evolved to expedite workflow. You need to be continually examining all processes, policies and systems which impact on the customer and looking for ways to make them less burdensome from the customer's perspective. Management's role in the development and implementation of improvement plans must be strong, and highly visible. Sustained quality improvement efforts require the highest level of commitment from managers and continual attention and action. This commitment must be demonstrated through their actions.

Any system that wasn't designed for the essential purpose of creating a high level of customer satisfaction rarely, if ever, results in high levels of customer satisfaction… no matter how hard employees try!

Employees at all levels of the organization must be actively involved in the implementation of improvement plans. Managers play a critical role in identifying and removing barriers to the delivery of service excellence. Minor improvements can be perceived as major improvements by the customer.

Encourage your staff to constantly look for better, faster and unique ways of doing business in a way that your customers value and enable your staff to make these changes or communicate the changes required to those who are empowered to do so.

Ask yourself the following questions. Jot down what you need to do differently, based on your answers.

1. Do I demonstrate, by my actions, a desire to align our systems towards service excellence?

2. What have I done to ensure that each of my people is continually seeking better, faster and different ways of doing their jobs? What do I do to encourage this?

3. How am I involving all my staff in continuous improvement efforts?

4. Listen to the Voice of the Customer

Listening to customers and continually realigning systems and actions to what customers want and need is critical. While periodic customer surveys are important, listening to the customer should be a routine part of day-to-day business practices especially at the point of contact with customers. We will address this issue in greater detail in the Know Your Customer and Learning

Customer-Focused Leadership

From the Customer chapters. Enable every customer-contact person to truly listen to what customers say and don't say. Recognize that customers' perceptions are their reality. Create processes to catalogue your customer perceptions and act on this intelligence by aligning your operational practices wherever possible to positively impact on your customers' perceptions. Customers also make sweeping conclusions about product quality and service based on minor details, so pay attention to the little things.

Action

Ask yourself the following questions. Jot down what you need to do differently, based on your answers.

1. What mechanisms have I put in place to help my people gather information about the perceptions of our customers?

2. What mechanisms have I put in place to help my people gather information about the perceptions of our internal business partners?

3. How do I use this information?

4. What expectations have I communicated to my staff regarding assessing our performance from our customers' point of view?

5. Lead with a Customer Focus

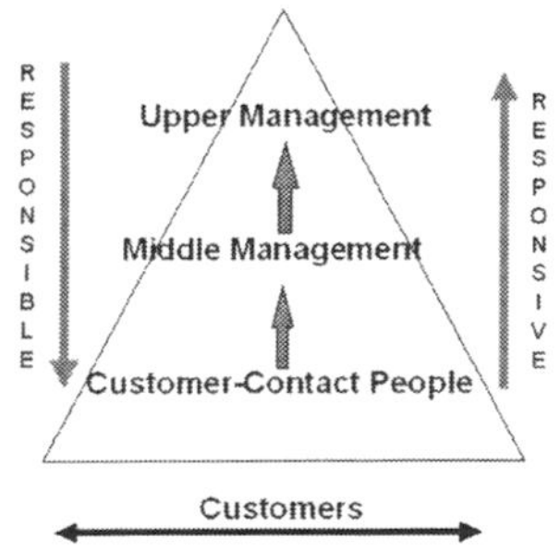

Like most organizations, you probably have a *Responsive Up Mind-Set* where upper management is responsible for setting and communicating the organization's vision, direction and goals. In this structure the frontline and support staff are responsive to the needs of middle management who are responsive to the needs of upper management. This is illustrated in figure 1.

A Customer-Focused Leader's goal is to combine this with *The Service Mind-Set* which is depicted in figure 2.

The Service Mind-Set inverts this structure so that upper management views itself as serving the needs of middle management who service the needs of the frontline and support staff who in turn service the needs of the customer. This is the mind-set that supports leadership with a customer focus. This means seeing yourself as a service organization for your employees.

Recognize that excellent service is impossible if you over-control. Understand that people are generally eager to do a good job and distressed when they can't. Remember that frustrated employees do not deliver good service.

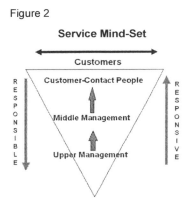

Figure 1
Responsive Up Mind-Set

Figure 2
Service Mind-Set

Customer-Focused Leadership

View your staff as your customers while at the same time become very adept at managing paradox such as "How can my subordinate be my customer?" or, "How can I increase customer focus while looking for ways to exercise fiscal restraint?"

Action

Ask yourself the following questions. Jot down what you need to do differently, based on your answers.

1. Do I over-control my people, limiting their ability to respond to customers' needs quickly and creatively?

2. What are some ways I can improve the quantity and quality of customer information my employees receive?

3. What have I done to create a service mind-set?

6. Define Service Boundaries

Each employee needs to understand your organization's service values and be able to connect these values to everyday actions. A leader must define a performance playing field that will allow employees to handle the routine deviations from normal customer transactions or interactions. The employee's performance playing field must be wide enough to allow employees to handle all routine transactions and interactions, as well as the predictable and routine deviations they face, and narrow enough to protect the financial integrity of the business operation. Each employee must have clearly defined goals, boundaries and guidelines which enable him or her to deliver quality service. It must be clear how achieving performance goals will contribute to service quality.

Setting effective service goals requires that every employee thoroughly understands the basic promise your company makes to your customers and Moments of Truth (this is covered in Learning from the Customer) for which he or she is responsible and can identify how to impress the customer. The customer-focused leader creates a service playing field that allows people to succeed. Clearly define measurable and achievable goals and boundaries based on employee capabilities and guidelines to enable them to deliver quality service.

Action

Ask yourself the following questions. Jot down what you need to do differently, based on your answers.

1. How have I translated our corporate values into reality for my staff?

2. When setting performance goals with my people, how are our customers brought into the equation?

3. When setting performance goals with my people, how are our internal business partners brought into the equation?

4. What have I done to ensure that my employees clearly understand my department's service goals and standards?

Customer-Focused Leadership

7. Provide Autonomy

Every employee needs to understand why what he or she does is important in the context of service quality. Ensure that every employee has the requisite knowledge and skill relative to their specific job function combined with a clear understanding of the playing field. When employees demonstrate this understanding and these capabilities, give them the autonomy to take action; set them up for success, not failure.

The people with the most customer contact are the best source of information regarding the customers' needs and wants. The people with the most internal business partner contact are the best source of information regarding their needs and wants. So don't micro-manage. When people show they can do their job, then let them do the job. Too many rules make it difficult, if not impossible, for service providers to effectively perform their jobs. Rules and procedures designed to protect against a small percentage of individuals convey a message of mistrust to the majority of honest customers. Replace rules with judgment.

Action

Ask yourself the following questions. Jot down what you need to do differently, based on your answers.

1. When was the last time I identified an obstacle to service quality and did something about it?
2. Have I established rules, policies or procedures which limit my people's ability to provide service excellence?
3. Do I encourage my staff to take an active role in identifying and removing obstacles?
4. What barriers do I put in my employees' way?
5. Do I stand behind my employees' decisions even when they are different from what I would have done as long as they benefit the customer?

8. Measure What's Important

Some say "You get what you measure." ... The reality is... "You get what you pay attention to." A major responsibility of a leader is to create effective and accurate measures from the customer's perspective. Good measurement allows employees to understand how to be successful within the organization. You can do this by translating these measures into actions that will allow employees to understand what good service looks like and how to succeed.

Measurement is about paying attention to the service performance you want, and focusing on outcomes rather than activities. Set service performance goals that are realistic while at the same time strive to go beyond the basics in an effort to exceed customers' expectations. Ensure that every employee understands and agrees to what is being measured, why it is important and how these measures reflect the defined playing field. The scorecard you use to assess success must be developed from the customer's point of view.

Customer-Focused Leadership

| Action |

Ask yourself the following questions. Jot down what you need to do differently, based on your answers.

1. Do I pay attention to the tasks my employees perform or to the outcomes of their performance?

2. What have I done to ensure that my employees understand how their performance is evaluated?

3. When assessing my employees' performance, do I see it through the eyes of their customers or internal business partners?

4. How do I gather information regarding my employees' customers' points-of-view?

9. Accountability for All

You have an obligation to your customers, to employees, and to the company to be unwavering in your demands for service excellence. Employees will pay more attention if they know they will be provided with solid, equitable and constructive positive feedback on their performance. Employees give credibility to service quality if they are held accountable to the outcomes of their performance.

Measurement must be followed by action. Action means giving timely feedback on both good service performance and poor service performance, equally. Provide feedback as close to the service performance occurrence as possible. A lack of action communicates that service is not important, individual performance does not make a difference, there are no clear-cut performance expectations, and that the organization's leadership is not credible. Pleasing the customer is the only valid end result of service performance.

| Action |

Ask yourself the following questions. Jot down what you need to do differently, based on your answers.

1. Do I hold my people accountable for the end results vs. activities?

2. Do I avoid dealing with instances of poor performance?

3. Would my people say that "No news is good news"? That is, do I give feedback only on negative performance?

Customer-Focused Leadership

10. Recognize and Reward

Successful service leaders ensure attention is paid to those who serve customers well and to those who assist in that effort. They show their appreciation to those who make sure the organization's customers are served properly. Consistent recognition of achievement is an integral part of building and maintaining a customer-focused culture. A good work environment depends on positive feedback, so "Catch people doing things right."

Good leadership makes a big deal of little things and thereby creates a performance culture where little things become a big deal. Recognize the desired changes in service behavior you want frequently and provide rewards when you have seen a sustained improvement in service performance outcomes. Ensure employees know what they need to do to earn a reward. Provide rewards that are valued from the employees' perspective and ensure that you reward those who deserve it.

Ask yourself the following questions. Jot down what you need to do differently, based on your answers.

1. Do I consistently recognize all of my employees' achievements?
2. Do I have service performance standards embedded in my performance management system?
3. How do I celebrate small accomplishments?
4. How frequently does my group or team hold celebrations?

Built on a solid foundation of dynamic internal service your goal must be to master the effective use of all these key Customer-Focused Leadership fundamentals.

How Customer Focused are you?

Would you like to know? As a bonus for buying this book, we invite you to complete a complimentary online self-assessment to help you determine this. E-mail us, provide the following code: OUMG1952, and we'll send you a link to the assessment

Customer-Focused Leadership

You may recall that one of the research findings we mentioned was that CFO's recognized that Customer Satisfaction was a reflection of Employee Satisfaction.

You could have perfect processes and policies but if employees weren't motivated, recognized and committed to the cause, service would suffer.

A significant pay-off of ensuring that all managers are effectively trained to be customer-focused leaders is that the management skills and leadership styles required to become customer-focused are the same ones that contribute to higher levels of employee satisfaction.

- Positively impacts on customer satisfaction

- Reduces employee turnover

- Reduces absenteeism and health related absences

- Improves employee productivity

- Reduces the costs associated with re-work and operational inefficiencies

- Creates a wealth of organizational knowledge and expertise

- Makes coming to work more enjoyable

Training your managers to be Customer-Focused Leaders is not the only thing that needs to be done however. Throughout this book we will explore issues related to aligning your systems to be more customer-focused. This also includes aligning your internal policies and practices relating to employee related issues such as:

- Your performance management system (job descriptions, performance reviews etc.)

- Salary structures and practices, promotion criteria and possibilities

- Reward and recognition programs

- Employee benefits programs

While we will not be elaborating on these topics in great detail in this book, it is essential that you take actions which your employees value and which your employees consider to be fair and equitable.

Customer-Focused Leadership

My Thoughts on the Questions Posed

Commit to Service Excellence

Be Pro-Active in Recovery

Enhance and Align your Systems

Listen to the Voice of the Customer

Lead with a Customer Focus

Define Service Boundaries

Provide Autonomy

Measure What's Important

Accountability for All

Recognize and Reward

Customer-Focused Leadership

"Excellence is not an act, it's a habit.'
- Aristotle

Know Your Customer

Chapter 6

Characteristics of Successful Customer-Focused Organizations:

"Aligned their processes and procedures to ensure a quality customer experience."

Before you can align your systems, processes and procedures you need to know what your customers want and expect. You need to listen to the voice of the customer.

Customer-focused organizations become very good at listening to the voice of their customers because they truly want to know what they value.

If you drink the occasional beer there's a good chance you have heard of The Miller Brewing Company. What you may not know is that they were the first to create lite beer. This story illustrates the importance of knowing your customers and the impact that customer perceptions have on their expectations and your business.

> *The brewing industry is enormously profitable and highly competitive. Many years ago, Miller came up with a brand new concept: "Lite Beer". The timing was perfect. The market was looking for a product which was believed to be less fattening yet still attractive to avid beer drinkers. With their new product ready, Miller hit the market with a major ad campaign. Some of you may recall it. "Drink Miller Lite, it has 30% fewer calories." Production was in full force and shelves were stocked everywhere with this new, sure to win product. There was just one problem. People were not buying it! The Company was in a quandary. This was the best thing since sliced bread but it wasn't selling.*

> *In a panic, their marketing team stood back and reassessed their situation. They knew that their primary customer was not the individual who would belly up to the bar and say "Look at this, this beer has 30% fewer calories". They reminded themselves that their customer was the one they affectionately referred to as a "caser". Caser's were easy to recognize. They were the ones who bought beer by the pitcher, not the glass. The marketing team spent time analyzing what was important to their customers and what their customers' perceptions were of their new product. What they finally came up with was the longest running and most successful ad campaign in their history. You might remember it. "Drink Miller Lite. Tasters Great, Less Filling." To their customer this was a gift from heaven. To a caser, this message was saying, it tastes great and most importantly, you can drink more! Needless to say, lite beer took off and soon all the other breweries were scrambling to create their own.*

By truly knowing their customers, finding out what was important to them and tapping into their perceptions, the company was incredibly successful.

Here's another example.

A large consumer bank (name withheld because lawyers are expensive) was looking for ways to cut operational expenses and boost its profitability. Since this bank supported a large branch network (nearly 1200 offices) the payroll expense to support the branch network was very high. Bank executives decided they would reduce headcount by offering its customers more self-service options. Rather than the traditional branch design where several bank tellers served customers, they decided to offer PC/Internet banking, tele-banking, manual deposits / ATM's and on-line product catalogues in each branch.

Know Your Customer

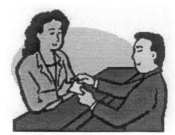

Instead of a full staff of tellers there was one teller and one host/hostess whose job it was to gently and patiently usher customers to the self-service banking options. It seemed like a good idea: cut staff by providing customers with the tools to bank on their own. The bank invested millions in the redesign.

The results were disastrous. At this point in time the bank had underestimated the importance of personal service. Customers preferred to speak with someone directly. They were more secure making financial transactions and getting answers from a person rather than a machine. Many of the bank's customers were elderly, wary of the automated services, and found the high-tech approach intimidating. Long lines formed as customers were funneled to a single teller. Complaints skyrocketed, new accounts dropped and some long-standing customers took their business elsewhere. After six months the bank had to hire back thousands of tellers and begin a campaign to repair its damaged reputation.

This chapter:

- outlines the importance of listening to the voice of the customer
- offers a simple method to better understand your customers and their needs
- provides sample surveys and customer interview tools
- explains important considerations when designing your survey process
- assists you in designing your own survey instrument

Why is this important?

What's the cost of an unhappy customer? Consider these statistics from a study conducted by the White House Office of Consumer Affairs:

- 96 percent of unsatisfied customers never complain about poor service BUT;
- Over 90 percent of those unsatisfied customers will never patronize the offending business again AND;
- Each of those dissatisfied customers will tell their story to an average of nine people AND;
- 13 percent of those dissatisfied customers will tell their story to more than twenty people!

Let's put this into context. Out of 25 people, if you get 1 complaint, that means that 23 people didn't bother. Out of those, 21 won't come back. And they will tell between 190 and 200 people how bad you were. That means you will have at least 190 people telling others how bad your service is. And all you got was ONE complaint. So what would happen if you got 10 complaints in a day? What about in a week? What about in a month? You get the point.

The next section describes attributes that customers commonly use to evaluate products, services and your service. In addition, you'll find a creative exercise that walks you through the experience of being your customer.

Know Your Customer

Be the Customer

Action

Before you can approach customers for their feedback on your products, services and service you need to develop a sensitivity to service quality yourself. It can be very difficult to objectively critique your own service (but we'll show you how later) so an easier place to start is to focus on your own attitude as a customer. For example, think about some of your experiences as a customer, such as:

- eating at a restaurant
- dealing with a credit card billing problem
- purchasing a home or vehicle
- a healthcare situation

- retail shopping
- dealing with phone companies or utilities
- calling a government office or agency
- enrolling at a college or paying tuition
- handling an insurance problem

What was it specifically that made your experience especially positive or negative? Here are a list of typical service related issues that may get you thinking:

Negative	Positive
Service associate uses a rude or impatient tone of voice	Service associate is congenial and takes time to explain product or service
Non-verbal behavior of service associate conveys lack of interest or concern	Non-verbal behavior suggests service associate is attentive and focused on the customer's issue
Service associate provides the bare minimum in terms of service support	Service associate offers advice or options beyond the customer's immediate buying experience
Service assistance is difficult to access (i.e. no service associate available, phone line busy or extended wait time, transferred among individuals, inconvenient service locations)	Service assistance is readily available to the customer
Customer fails to get an answer to a service issue or fails to get an adequate explanation of options for solving service issues	Customer gets satisfactory resolution to a service issue or is given a clear explanation of options for resolving a problem
Product or service fails or is difficult to use	Product or service works reliably and is easy to use
Product or service is expensive compared to alternatives	Product or service is priced competitively and offers a good value
Service ends when the sales transaction ends	Service representative provides follow-up to ensure customer is satisfied with the product or service

Know Your Customer

Service SatisFactors

We discussed what customers want when it comes to service in Chapter 1. Let's turn this theory into actionable steps. We have taken the liberty of translating these service dimensions into five easily identifiable service factors which we call SatisFactors. These SatisFactors will make it easier for you to determine what you want and expect as a customer and then, what your customers want and expect.

Service Cosmetics Are service associates friendly and empathic to the customer's needs (service-oriented)?

Service Accuracy Can customers get an accurate answer to their questions (same answer each time from each person)?

Service Accessibility Is it easy for a customer to get service?

Product/Service Reliability Does the product or service the customer purchased work as intended?

Cost Competitive Is the product or service priced competitively?

Action

In the Be the Customer section above you evaluated your own experience as a customer. Now it's time think about your customers and the products and/or services and service you provide.

What does your Customer expect?

The following exercise will help you document your thoughts. **This is an excellent exercise for all your employees.** Use it to facilitate a discussion of service factors you must focus on to satisfy your customers.

Know Your Customer

Be the Customer

Step 1: Anticipate your customer's expectations. What specifically should you deliver to satisfy a customer who purchases your product or service?

SatisFactors	To satisfy our customers' expectations
Service Cosmetics – service associates should be friendly and empathic to customer needs (service-oriented)	Actions:
Service Accuracy – customer should get an accurate answer to his/her question or a clear explanation of alternatives (same answer each time from each person)	Actions:
Service Accessibility – should be easy for customer to get service and assistance	Actions:
Product/Service Reliability – product or service should work as intended. If not, problem should be handled quickly and to the satisfaction of the customer.	Actions:
Cost Competitive – product or service should be priced competitively	Actions:

Know Your Customer

Step 2: Now for each situation and satisfactors you identified, what can you do to exceed the customer's expectations?

Satisfactors	To exceed our customers' expectations
Service Cosmetics – service associates should be friendly and empathic to customer needs (service-oriented)	Actions:
Service Accuracy – customer should get an accurate answer to his/her question or a clear explanation of alternatives (same answer each time from each person)	Actions:
Service Accessibility – should be easy for customer to get service and assistance	Actions:
Product/Service Reliability – product or service should work as intended. If not, problem should be handled quickly and to the satisfaction of the customer	Actions:
Cost Competitive – product or service should be priced competitively	Actions:

Know Your Customer

Listening to the Voice of the Customer

So how do you gather feedback from your customers? The only way to be sure about what they are thinking is to ask them. Listening to the voice of your customers can be done formally through well designed surveys and interviews, or informally, every day by your staff.

Let's first consider the easiest and most cost effective method: day-to-day by your staff.

Some companies spend thousands, even millions of dollars to find out what their customers want, need and expect. Market research, focus groups, Customer Satisfaction Surveys all represent excellent tools to tap into the mind of the customer. But there is one source that is even more effective. You! You and everyone who works in your company. People who interact with customers daily, whether by phone or in person, are the perfect resource to gather important customer information. People in a support role who do not interact directly with the paying customer are also an important information gathering resource because they are part of the service delivery supply chain.

The questions you ask are critical. Sadly, many well-intentioned service providers ask the wrong questions. You've probably been asked these questions yourself or maybe you have even used some of them.

It is important that you ask the right kind of questions–questions that will give you specific information that can be used to make changes and improvements that customers find important and stop doing things that customers find annoying or inconsequential.

The right questions focus on what you need to start doing, stop doing and keep doing. We suggest that you make it easy for the customer to answer. You can do this by asking questions which allow the customer to focus on a small and specific area, rather than broad, general, closed-ended questions, which are typical of most "Wrong" questions.

Keep in mind that asking the right questions is only part of the equation. Being a good listener is essential. Listening is an essential service quality skill. If you are not prepared to truly listen to what the customer is saying, and if you are not prepared to act on the information you get, the questions you ask will be of little importance.

The Wrong Questions

- **How are we doing?**
- **Are you satisfied?**
- **Are you getting what you need?**
- **Is everything Okay?**

The right questions

- **If we could change one thing about the way we treat you, what would it be?**
- **What one thing can we do to make it easier to do business with us?**
- **Was this experience better than... (the last time, dealing with competitor)...?**
- **What do others do better?**

Know Your Customer

Customer Surveys

If you are going to use surveys as a means to listen to your customers be sure focus your questions on your strategic objectives. For example, are you concerned with product or service attributes?

Product Survey - Sample Questions

Product surveys tend to evaluate products or goods based on qualities such as....

- **effectiveness** – does the product work as it's supposed to?
- **reliability** – does the product work every time it's supposed to?
- **availability** – is the product easily accessible?
- **cost** – is the cost of the product reasonable?
- **ease of use** – is the product easy to use?

Service Survey - Sample Questions

Service surveys tend to evaluate services based on qualities such as...

- **effectiveness** – did the service provide the intended outcome?
- **courteousness** – was the service presented in a friendly manner?
- **timeliness** – was the service available in a timely manner?
- **ease of service** – was the service easy to use?
- **personalization** – was the service tailored to your specific needs?

It is essential that all the information you gather is catalogued and reviewed. Change those things you are empowered to immediately. Things that may require larger scale changes or approvals by decision makers should be passed along to the appropriate people so that they can be acted upon in the most effective way.

Last but not least you need to make customers feel like they're your most important concern every time they interact with your business.

Know Your Customer

Now let's dig deeper into how to develop and conduct formal surveys and interviews.

Conducting Formal Surveys and Interviews

In the Be the Customer exercise you completed you had an opportunity to consider what a customer should expect of your products, services and service. While you might be correct in your assumptions, how do you really know what is important to your customers unless you ask them?

Using formal surveys and customer telephone interviews and focus groups will enable you to verify your assumptions about your customers' expectations as well as learn what they really want.

Let's take a look at some sample surveys and tools from other business.

Sample Surveys

You will find below two sample surveys.

1. A Management Consulting Firm. This is a feedback survey for customers who participated in a Leadership Assessment process.

2. A Home Rentals Company. This is a satisfaction survey to assess patron satisfaction with home equipment rentals.

Know Your Customer

CUSTOMER SURVEY TOOL - MANAGEMENT CONSULTING COMPANY

You recently participated in a Leadership Assessment process intended to provide you with useful feedback and suggestions on how you can improve your management skills and also leverage your management strengths.

Please circle your rating of the following aspects of your experience.

Administrative support provided by our consultants	- Were instructions clear and easy to understand? - Did you receive instructions/answers in a timely manner?
	1 2 3 4 5 6 7 8 9 10 Poor Average Excellent
Usability of the online system	- Was it easy to use and navigate? - Was response time reasonable? - Did it take a reasonable amount of time to complete the assessment(s)?
	1 2 3 4 5 6 7 8 9 10 Poor Average Excellent
Content of the assessment	- Were questions clear and easy to interpret? - Were questions pertinent to your job?
	1 2 3 4 5 6 7 8 9 10 Poor Average Excellent
Individual reporting package	- Was the report easy to understand? - Did the report provide a useful analysis of the data?
	1 2 3 4 5 6 7 8 9 10 Poor Average Excellent
Individual feedback session	- Did you receive useful information and/or support from our consultant? - Did our consultant demonstrate expert knowledge of management competencies? - Did our consultant offer practical suggestions on how you could improve your management skills? - Were supporting materials and exercises in your follow-up session useful?
	1 2 3 4 5 6 7 8 9 10 Poor Average Excellent
The assessment process overall	- Did you receive useful feedback from peers, direct reports, your manager, etc.? - Did you gain insights on how/where you can improve?
	1 2 3 4 5 6 7 8 9 10 Poor Average Excellent

Narrative Feedback

Please provide at least one suggestion for how we could improve our Leadership Assessment process:

Know Your Customer
CUSTOMER SURVEY - HOME RENTALS

Neighborhood Rentals Customer Satisfaction Survey

Neighborhood Rentals is committed to ensuring your total satisfaction with our products and services. In order to constantly improve our business we would like your feedback on your recent visit. Please take a moment to complete this brief survey. In return you'll receive a coupon for $10.00 off your next rental.

Thank you for your patronage and your valuable feedback!   Please circle the appropriate response:

1. How would you rate the customer service at Neighborhood Rentals?	• Did an associate greet you promptly? • Was the associate friendly and attentive? • Did an associate help load your rental equipment?
1 2 3 4 5 6 7 8 9 10 Poor Average Excellent	
.2. How would you rate our product knowledge?	• Did an associate explain how to operate your rental equipment? • Did an associate explain safety considerations for your rental equipment? • Did an associate explain what to do in an event there's a problem with your rental equipment?
1 2 3 4 5 6 7 8 9 10 Poor Average Excellent	
3. How would you rate our selection of rental equipment at Neighborhood Rentals?	• Were you able to find the equipment you needed? • Did the equipment we offered have all options you needed?
1 2 3 4 5 6 7 8 9 10 Poor Average Excellent	
4. How would you rate our prices at Neighborhood Rentals?	• Do you think the cost was reasonable for the equipment you rented? • How does Neighborhood Rental compare to other rental services in terms of price?
1 2 3 4 5 6 7 8 9 10 Poor Average Excellent	
5. How would you rate the reliability of our rental equipment at Neighborhood Rentals?	• Did your rental equipment work properly? • Was your rental equipment easy to use?
1 2 3 4 5 6 7 8 9 10 Poor Average Excellent	
6. How likely is it you will patronize Neighborhood Rentals the next time you need rental equipment?	
1 2 3 4 5 6 7 8 9 10 Not Likely Average Very Likely	
Comments/Suggestions for Improvement:	

Please return your survey to any Neighborhood Rental store or drop it in the mail to receive your coupon for $10.00 off your next rental purchase.   Thank You!

Customer Name:	Street Address:
City/State/Zip	Telephone:

Know Your Customer

Sample Interview Tools

You will find below two sample interview tools. The first is patient feedback on an office visit to a Healthcare provider. It was conducted by a Business Office representative. The second is a Customer Feedback form on shopping experience at an upscale retailer. It is a brief interview conducted by the store supervisor/manager.

CUSTOMER INTERVIEW TOOL - HEALTHCARE

Background: This interview tool is used by personnel in the Business Office of the Morris, Hague and Moriarty Pediatric Clinic to gather patient / parent feedback after an office visit. If the interview is not conducted immediately after the visit, a follow-up phone call is conducted within 48 hours.

Morris, Hague and Moriarty Pediatric Clinic

Patient / Parent Satisfaction Interview

Patient name:	Parent/Custodian:
Purpose of visit:	Physician/Nurse:
Date of visit:	Date of interview:

Was the parent/custodian able to get an appointment in a timely manner? If no, how long did it take?	Yes	No
Was the patient/custodian satisfied with the intake/administrative/insurance processes? If no, why?	Yes	No
Was the patient/parent/custodian satisfied with the attention/manner in which the attending physician/nurse conducted him/herself? If no, why?	Yes	No
Is the patient/parent/custodian comfortable/confident in the course of treatment recommended by the attending physician/nurse? If no, why?	Yes	No
Does the patient/parent/custodian have any suggestions on how we can improve our practice? If yes, please document details.	Yes	No
Would the patient/parent/custodian like a follow-up phone call? If yes, please document best time of day and phone number.	Yes	No

Be sure to thank the parent/custodian for their feedback and for selecting Morris, Hague and Moriarty as their primary healthcare provider.

Know Your Customer

CUSTOMER INTERVIEW TOOL - RETAIL

Background: Devon's is a specialty Home Decorating Center that caters to clientele with above average size/cost homes. Because Devon's clientele tend to be individuals with incomes well above average, their customer base is smaller but spends more per purchase. The manager of Devon's insisted on an interview format rather than a survey to keep the process personable. Store supervisors were trained to conduct in-store or after purchase interviews with randomly selected patrons.

Devon's Home Decorating Center
Customer Feedback Interview

Was Devon's able to provide you with the furnishings and/or decorating needs you were looking for?

Would you like Devon's to carry any furnishings or decorating services you didn't find today?

Were you satisfied with every aspect of our service today?

Is there anything we could have done to make your shopping experience more pleasurable?

NOTE: If customer has any complaint, comment, or suggestion that requires follow-up, ask if we could call them or send a service representative to their home.

The next section provides step-by-step details to make sure your survey is a success.

Know Your Customer

Designing a Survey / Interview Process

For clarity, the next two sections will differentiate between the *process* of administering a survey and the *instrument* itself.

a) Determining the right type of survey

b) Administration

c) Incentives

a) Determining the right type of survey

If you want to gather customer feedback you'll need to decide which approach is best for your type of business – paper survey, online survey or interview. Here are some considerations:

Volume	If your business handles a high volume of customers, e.g., retail or restaurant, then a paper survey or online process is usually better since you want to solicit a fairly representative sample of customers for feedback. Conducting an in-store interview or telephone interview with a high volume of customers can be logistically difficult.
Product/Service Complexity	If your service or product is fairly complex or requires specialized knowledge, e.g., healthcare or law services, an interview format may be more appropriate than a survey. Customers may have questions or require clarification on questions that paper surveys cannot accommodate.
Service Distinction	If personalized service is a critical business driver for your business, then consider using an interview process for obtaining feedback. Paper surveys and online surveys are obviously less personable and certainly more common than an interview. This will support your effort to distinguish your business in terms of personalized service.
Cost	Paper-based surveys tend to be more expensive since you will incur desktop publishing, printing and mail costs. Both types, paper and interview will require resources for data analysis. Online surveys eliminate the paper and processing time but it is sometimes difficult to get your customers to go online. You also will incur costs associated with the development of the instrument but there are many providers now who can help you.
Type of Feedback	Paper and online surveys are more effective at presenting scaled questions – i.e. "On a scale of 1-10 please rate our service." This type of data is called *quantitative* data since it can be aggregated into averages and distributions. An interview is more effective at gathering *qualitative* data since the interviewer can ask open-ended questions and probe customers for details. For example, rather than asking:

"Did you enjoy your visit today?" (Yes or No)

an open-ended question could be posed as:

"What did you enjoy about your visit today?" (open-ended)

Quantitative data is easier to summarize if you are dealing with a high volume of responses. Qualitative data takes longer to summarize since you need to review narrative feedback, but you're likely to get more detailed feedback. A great benefit of online surveys over paper is that you will get the results faster and in real time.

Know Your Customer

Other Considerations which factor into the Design

Rating Scales

If you're using a rating scale for your questions, we recommend you use a scale of 1 - 10, with 1 representing the most negative response, and 10 representing the most positive response:

How would you rate the reliability of our products?

1	2	3	4	5	6	7	8	9	10
Very Unreliable				Average					Excellent

This design does two things. First, respondents can easily decipher the anchors (most negative and most positive responses). Second, using an even number of options (ten) forces the recipient to choose a more negative (1, 2 3, 4 or 5) or more positive response (6, 7, 8, 9, or 10). More than ten options will make it difficult for recipients to differentiate among numbers and responses start to cluster around average. Some designers prefer a six point scale. This can work equally well depending on the information you wish to gather.

Provide criterion

When asking a customer to comment on some aspect of your business, you will get more reliable answers if you provide *criterion* for each question. For example, suppose you're gathering customer feedback on your Internet Training product. Your survey could ask a survey recipient to:

Rate the usability of the online training system

1	2	3	4	5	6	7	8	9	10
Poor					Average				Excellent

Or, it could ask:

Rate the usability of the online training system

- Was it easy to use and navigate?
- Was response time reasonable?

1	2	3	4	5	6
Poor		Average		Excellent	

The second option will yield more reliable results since you've provided recipients some common criterion by which to assess the online training system. The point is, when you ask someone to rate the quality of your service, the reliability of your products, the responsiveness of your service department, etc., tell them what you mean by specifying criterion.

Open-ended comments

Always provide at least one open-ended comments question in case a recipient has a suggestion or comment that doesn't exactly fit your other questions. For example:

Do you have any other comments on your shopping experience?

Please list any other issues or comments.

General comments/suggestions

Seek negative feedback

Some recipients will be reluctant to provide negative feedback especially if you're conducting a face-to-face interview or a telephonic interview. Unfortunately that's exactly the feedback you'll benefit from the most. In order to encourage recipients to give honest, critical feedback, ask questions like:

What was the most negative aspect of your shopping experience?

Please provide at least one suggestion for how we could improve our service.

What would have made your dining experience more pleasurable?

Know Your Customer

b) Administration

The next consideration is *how* to administer your survey. Let's review all three types of surveys.

Administering paper surveys

If you're administering a paper survey it can be done in one of three ways:

1. **Completed in-store/house**
2. **Delivered in-store/returned later**
3. **Mailed to customer/returned later**

1. Completed in-store

Example: At Here's to Your Health, a home fitness retail chain, service representatives ask customers to complete a brief paper survey at the time they pay for their purchase. Customers are told if they complete the survey they will receive a coupon for ten percent off their next purchase. A semi-private area is set up on the counter so the customer can complete the survey in confidence. Completed surveys are put into a locked survey box and retrieved after hours.

Pros	Cons
Saves on postage and administrative effort of mailing surveys	Requires some area for customer to complete the survey in privacy
Typically results in a slightly higher return rate than other paper-based surveys	Only get feedback from customers who purchased a product – miss valuable feedback from customers who leave without making a purchase
Experience is fresh in customer's mind so details are easy to remember	Extends check out time for customers

How to administer a "Completed in-store" survey

- Develop the paper-based survey.
- Set up a private area to complete the survey and a drop box.
- Determine if any incentive will be offered.
- Train employees on how to present the survey to customers.
- Determine how surveys will be assigned (i.e., to all customers, to customers during scheduled times/days, etc.). This may depend on the volume you deal with.
- Determine who will review and summarize the surveys, how often and what will be done with the feedback.
- Review the survey process periodically to determine if it can be improved or if the survey itself should be changed.

Know Your Customer

2. Delivered in-store/returned later

Example: Neighborhood Rentals, a chain of home rental stores, gives a customer satisfaction survey to each person who makes a purchase at one of its locations. Whenever possible store managers also give surveys to customers who shop but leave without making a purchase. Customers are told they will receive a coupon for 10% off their next rental if they return the survey. Customers can take the survey home and return it by mail (or in person). If customers return the survey by mail the store sends them a discount coupon via mail.

Pros	Cons
Can gather feedback from customers who do not make a purchase (price? selection? service?)	More expensive than in-store surveys since postage is required to mail surveys and discount coupons
Does not extend customer check out time	More expensive than in-store surveys since many are not returned (increased cost of materials)
Does not require special area for customers to complete the survey in privacy	Since time may lapse between shopping experience and completing the survey – customer may forget important details

How to administer a "Delivered in-store/returned later" survey

- Develop the paper-based survey and a return mail envelope.
- Call the Post Office to determine most cost effective means for returning surveys.
- Determine if any incentive will be offered.
- Train employees on how to present the survey to customers.
- Determine how surveys will be assigned (i.e., to all customers, to customers during scheduled times/days, etc.). This may depend on the volume you deal with.
- Determine who will review and summarize the surveys, how often and what will be done with the feedback.
- Review the survey process periodically to determine if it can be improved or if the survey itself should be changed.

Know Your Customer

3. Mailed to customer / returned later

Example: Holston Group Insurance Services mails a customer satisfaction survey to new clients when they buy an insurance policy. Address information is gathered at the time a policy is opened and used to send out the survey. A return envelope is included in the mailer to make it easy for the policyholder to return the survey. (Note: Unless you regularly gather customer address information during the course of the purchase do not use this method. Asking a customer for their address simply to send them a survey will inconvenience the customer.)

Pros	Cons
Does not lengthen the customer shopping or on-line purchasing time	More expensive than in-store surveys since postage is required to mail surveys and, if applicable, discount coupons
	More expensive than in-store surveys since many are not returned (increased cost of materials)
Does not require special area for customers to complete the survey in privacy	Only get feedback from customers who purchased a product – miss valuable feedback from customers who shop without making a purchase
	Since time may lapse between shopping experience and completing the survey – customer may forget important details

How to administer a "Mailed to customer/returned later" survey

- Develop the paper-based survey and a return mail envelope.
- Call the Post Office to determine most cost effective means for mailing / returning surveys.
- Determine if any incentive will be offered.
- Determine a process for mailing surveys.
- Determine how surveys will be assigned (i.e., to all customers, to customers during scheduled times/days, etc.). This may depend on the volume you deal with.
- Determine who will review and summarize the surveys, how often and what will be done with the feedback.
- Review the survey process periodically to determine if it can be improved or if the survey itself should be changed.

Know Your Customer

Administering Interviews

If you're administering an interview process for feedback it can be done in one of two ways:

1. **Completed in-store**
2. **Completed via telephone at a later date**

1. Completed in-store

Example: At Beckley's Auto Emporium, a service associate conducts brief on-site interviews with customers. The service associate will approach individuals as they are leaving the showroom or lot and ask if they have two minutes to complete a brief interview. In return they get a coupon for a free popcorn and soda at a nearby movie theatre. The service associate attempts to complete a minimum number of interviews per day. That number is based on the typical average of visitors per day (varies per weekday).

Pros	Cons
Saves on postage and administrative effort of mailing surveys	Requires a dedicated resource to conduct interviews
Allows for more detailed feedback since interviewer can use probing questions with customer	Typically requires more time to summarize data than paper-based surveys since narrative feedback takes more time to analyze than numeric ratings
Tends to emphasize a business's customer commitment leaving customers with a favorable impression of the business	Customers tend to avoid giving negative feedback in face-to-face interviews

How to administer a "Completed in-store" interview

- Develop a script or format for interview questions.
- Determine if any incentive will be offered.
- Train service representative on how to present the interview and use probing questions.
- Determine how interview candidates will be selected (i.e., certain number of customers per day). This may depend on the volume you deal with.
- Determine who will review and summarize the interview feedback, how often and what will be done with the feedback.
- Review the interview process periodically to determine if it can be improved or if the interview itself should be changed.

Know Your Customer

2. Completed via telephone at a later date

Example: ExecuNet provides private computer consulting, installation and training for executive managers who have limited time. ExecuNet provides 24 hour support tailored to an executive manager's busy life style. After services are rendered (typically at a manager's work place or home) the Vice President of ExecuNet conducts a follow-up phone interview to ensure the manager is completely satisfied with his or her service. (Note: Unless you regularly gather customer telephone information during the course of the purchase do not use this method. Asking a customer for their telephone number simply to conduct a survey will inconvenience the customer or be seen as intrusive.)

Pros	Cons
Saves on postage and administrative effort of mailing surveys	Requires a dedicated resource to conduct interviews
Allows for more detailed feedback since interviewer can use probing questions with customer	Typically requires more time to summarize data than paper-based surveys since narrative feedback takes more time to analyze than numeric ratings
Tends to emphasize a business's customer commitment leaving customers with a favorable impression of the business	Customers tend to avoid giving negative feedback although telephone interviews are better than face-to-face interviews in this respect.
Can be scheduled at a customer's convenience rather than taking additional time on site	Since time may lapse between shopping/services and completing the interview – customers may forget important details

How to administer a "Completed via telephone at a later date" interview

- Develop a script or format for interview questions.
- Determine if any incentive will be offered.
- Train service representative(s) on how to present interview and use probing questions.
- Determine how/when interview candidates will be contacted (i.e., certain number of customers per day). This may depend on the volume you deal with.
- Determine who will review and summarize the interview feedback, how often and what will be done with the feedback.
- Review the interview process periodically to determine if it can be improved or if the interview itself should be changed.

Know Your Customer

Administering Online Surveys

Most online surveys are administered via a company's website. While some companies have attempted to get their customers to go online in their place of business, most customers do not want to take the time even for short surveys. The challenge then becomes, how do you get the customer to go to your website? The best method we have seen is where companies build a large data base of customer names and email addresses and they get their customers permission to send out promotional email from time to time. Getting permission is very important. Remember how you feel when you are picking up email and have to contend with what you consider to be spam. Sending follow-up emails after a customer transaction to find out how the customer was treated can work well provided you don't inundate the customer after every sale. You can also offer incentives as discussed below to encourage customers to visit your website to provide feedback.

Pros	Cons
Saves on postage and administrative effort of mailing surveys	Requires a dedicated resource to manage surveys and website
Allows for more detailed feedback as open and closed questions can be used	More difficult to get customers to visit website to complete survey
Tends to emphasize a business's customer commitment leaving customers with a favorable impression of the business	Customers tend to avoid giving negative feedback unless they believe something will be done about it
Results are available in real time so you can act quickly when problems are identified	

Know Your Customer

Before you proceed:

There is one cardinal rule about asking your customers for feedback:

> **Don't ask them for feedback unless you are prepared to listen and initiate changes in how you operate your business!**

Customers often don't complain because they don't believe it will do any good. They will however tell you what they think if they believe you sincerely want to improve how you serve them.

c) Incentives

Typically you will get a higher completion and return rate on surveys and interviews based on two factors. First, your survey or interview process must be *easy and minimally inconvenient* to the customer. If it takes too long to complete or requires special information, customers will either avoid completing it or rush through and your results will be tainted. Second, if you provide an *incentive,* recipients are more likely to comply. If you are providing an incentive, be sure the incentive is significant enough to make it worth the customer's time but not so extravagant that it appears you're buying their feedback. Besides, spend too much and you'll go broke!

Types of Incentives

Survey Inserts – If you're mailing a survey to customers consider including a pen (makes it easier to complete and they get a gift) or some other insert like a mini calendar, bookmark etc. Marketing firms can assist you in identifying an appropriate insert and can offer volume discounts.

Coupons – Whether you're offering a paper-based, online or a telephone survey, consider including a discount coupon for a customer's next purchase. You'll encourage feedback and get them to return.

Recognition – Some companies recognize customers who provide truly unique or beneficial feedback by giving them public recognition. For instance, post their name (or even picture) in your store with their name and suggestion (Customer of the Month?). Once a month College Street Graphics takes out a small ad in the newspaper thanking customers for their feedback and ideas!

If you offer an incentive make sure the customer gets it. Don't wind up with egg on your face for failing to deliver.

Know Your Customer

Let's review briefly what you've covered to this point. You have:

- reviewed the most common "satisfactors" for customer service (cosmetics, accuracy, accessibility, reliability of products and services and cost)

- identified both positive and negative customer service experiences

- completed the Be the Customer exercise

- reviewed ways to listen to the voice of the customer

- reviewed samples of various customer surveys and interview tools

- reviewed important considerations for designing a customer survey process (type of survey, administration and incentives)

Now you're ready to design your own survey instrument. Remember, to do this, you'll need:

- to determine which type of survey instrument is best for your company (paper, online, interview or telephone)

- the results of your Be the Customer exercise

- to review the sample surveys and interview instruments to get ideas for designing your own instrument

- to determine the process for administering the survey or interview process

At the end of this chapter there is an exercise which you can use to help you develop a survey. Get together with some of your staff and discuss what you would like to accomplish. Review the information in this chapter with them and get their input. Then develop a survey and give it a try.

Know Your Customer

Now take a few minutes to complete the following exercise.

Exercise

6.2

Gathering Customer Feedback

STEP 1: **Determine which type of survey instrument is best for your company.**

Review the section, "Designing your own survey/interview process." Which type of survey will you use – paper, online, interview, or telephonic? Record your decision in the space provided below.

_____

_____

_____

_____

STEP 2: **Review the results of your Be the Customer exercise**

What actions did you identify for each of the satisfactors? (Refer to Step Two of that exercise.) How can each of those items be stated in such a way that a customer could assess your performance against them? For example, if you own a fast food restaurant one of your "satisfactors" would be how quickly you're able to serve the customer their food. That satisfactor might be stated as, "Customers should receive their order within three minutes of ordering their meal."

Comments:

_____

_____

_____

_____

_____

_____

Know Your Customer

Gathering Customer Feedback cont'd

STEP 3: **Review the sample surveys and interview instruments.**

Draft questions for your survey using the results of step 2 above. Draft your questions as open-ended questions or scaled questions (e.g.: If there was one thing we could have done better today when serving you or... on a scale of 1-10 rate our service...). Record your questions below.

_____

_____

_____

_____

_____

_____

_____

_____

_____

_____

_____

_____

_____

STEP 4: **Test your questions with one or more colleagues.**

Review your questions with colleagues or associates. Refine based on their feedback and then finalize.

Know Your Customer

Exercise

6.2

Gathering Customer Feedback cont'd

Step 5: **Determine a process for administering the survey or interview process.**

Consider the following questions and record your determinations below.

Paper-based or online surveys

Which method will you use - Completed in-store, Delivered in-store/returned later or Mailed to customer/returned later?

How will you select survey recipients?

Who will be responsible for administering or mailing the surveys?

If you're mailing surveys how will you obtain address information?

If recipients return surveys by mail how will you accommodate envelopes and postage?

If you're offering incentives for completing the survey what will they be? How will they be awarded?

Who will analyze and summarize survey results?

Interview or telephonic surveys

Which method will you use - Completed in-store or Completed via telephone at a later date?

How will you select interview candidates?

Who will be responsible for conducting the interview?

If you're conducting telephonic interviews how will you obtain telephone numbers?

If you're offering incentives for participating in the interview what will they be? How will they be awarded?

Who will analyze and summarize the interview results?

Conclusions:

_____

_____

_____

_____

_____

In summary, every business should have a process for gathering customer feedback. Without one, your business is operating blindly. Before you know it you will lose touch with the real preferences and needs of your customers and they will go elsewhere. Before we discuss what you need to do with the information you gather, there is something else to consider. You also need to know what your competition is doing so that you can ensure that your customers' experience with you is better than they would encounter with your competition.

Now That's Customer Focus!

Know Your Competition

Chapter 7

Characteristics of Successful Customer-Focused Organizations:

"Aligned their processes and procedures to ensure a quality customer experience."

It's probably hard to believe but Wal*Mart, the mega-retailer, started as a simple five-and-dime store. Sam Walton, whose family founded Wal*Mart was a man obsessed with studying his competition.

At the time, K Mart was the behemoth on the block. Walton viewed Kmart as his laboratory. He would visit the stores, make notes on their layout, interview employees and customers, at times under the watchful eye of curious managers wondering who this inquisitive young man was.

He took what worked at Kmart and used it to build his company. At the same time he learned from his competitors' mistakes and shortcomings, and used them too to grow his business. Imagine the reaction of those K Mart managers if they knew that this young man would grow a retailing empire unsurpassed by any competitor, including Kmart.

This chapter:

- provides unique techniques for gathering information about your competition

- provides an exercise to apply the techniques for gathering competitive information

- offers an exercise for producing a competition report card

Why is this important?

Obviously Wal*Mart has been tremendously successful, which is what makes this story such a powerful illustration of why knowing your competition is so critical. If you know the strengths and weaknesses of your competition, including what their customers like and don't like, you can use that to your advantage. You can advertise the unique benefits of your products versus theirs. You can constantly better them in terms of service. You can develop pricing strategies that make your business the obvious choice.

We realize that it's tough enough understanding your own business, let alone the competition. It is a lot of work, but you'll quickly realize the benefit.

The next section provides some creative techniques for gathering information about your competitors.

Know Your Competition

Gathering Competitive Information

Techniques for gathering competitive information include:

- **Product and service publications**
- **Customer solicitation**
- **"Shopping" the competition**
- **Independent evaluations**

Not all these approaches for gathering competitive information will work for every type of business. Choose and adapt the ones which fit your specific situation.

Product and service publications

The most obvious method of learning more about your competition is by product and service publications which they use for their marketing. Here are a few ways to get that information:

1. **Request product and service catalogues**	Call your competition and request any literature they have on their products and services. Sign up for any mailing lists they provide announcing new products or services.
2. **Visit their website**	If they have an Internet site check it out. Use it to submit inquiries and questions about their business.
3. **Buy a share of stock**	Obviously this will only work if your competition is a publicly traded firm. If you purchase a share of stock you will be sent an annual report on the company and can even attend shareholder meetings!

Customer solicitation

Wouldn't it be great to ask customers what they think of your competition? It can be done, but you need to be creative. Here are a few ways:

1. **Check out the Internet**	Many search engines can locate community forums on companies. For instance, go to Yahoo.com or Google.com and search on "Wal*mart." The search engine will return numerous articles on "Wal*mart" as well as a community forum where customers, employees, etc. can post questions and opinions on Wal*mart.
2. **Creative offerings**	Bailey's Engine and Autobody found itself fighting for survival among more established car repair shops including some national franchises. That's when John Bailey got creative. First, he ran a radio ad that told listeners if they brought in a receipt from another car repair shop they'd receive 10% off any service.

Know Your Competition

Customers dug up old receipts, cancelled checks and credit card statements to take advantage of the offer. Since they had the customer captive while repairs were being made, they asked them to complete a questionnaire that asked questions about the competition's service!

3. **Talk to your customers**

Ask your customers about their experiences. Have they dealt with your competition? If so, what did they think? Dawson's Jewelers claims "*an educated customer is our best customer.*" They'll actually recommend to shoppers that they compare the quality and cost of Dawson jewelry to other jewelers before making a purchase. That's confidence! This way they can constantly solicit feedback from their customers.

If you lose valued customers or customers that have been with you for some time, be sure to find out why they left. They can tell you much about your competition since their change in loyalty was probably not impulsive but rather done after some deliberation. If you maintain account history and notice a lack of activity by some customers, call them and find out if they're just not shopping for your products or services or if they've jumped ship. Some credit card companies will do that if they notice an account is dormant. Also – some oil & lube shops will call customers when it appears they've gone well past their 3,000 mile check without a visit. Did they forget or did they go elsewhere?

Action

"Shopping" the competition

In many industries such as banking and retail, it is a common practice to actually visit competitors as a potential customer. If you're going to compare your products and services to your competition use the exercise **Be the Customer** you completed in the **Know the Customer** chapter. In that exercise you produced a listing of customer commitments – or "satisfactors" you deemed important to providing quality service to your customers. Use those same "satisfactors" to gauge your competition!

Talk to their sales associates, customer service personnel – even management if applicable. Observe other customers. Are they receiving prompt, attentive service? Do they have questions about the products or services?

Know Your Competition

Independent evaluations

Sometimes using an objective, outside firm is the best approach for gathering really detailed competitive information. Here are some ideas:

Consumer reports	Check out consumer reports for information on your industry, products and the competition. You can also visit them on the Internet at <u>www.consumerreports.com</u>
Internet research	Search the Internet using keywords such as consumer protection, customer service, etc.
Better Business Bureau/Boards of Trade	Ask your Better Business Bureau or Board of Trade office for any information on the company you're investigating. They may share some information particularly if complaints or judgments have been filed against the company.
Industry journals and trade magazines	Many business fields have dedicated publications that talk about competition in the industry, new products, legislation impacting the industry, etc.
Competitive research	There are consulting firms who specialize in conducting competitive research using many of the above methods. Check your yellow pages under **management – consulting** for ones in your area.

Now you'll have a chance to try these techniques. In the next section is an exercise for applying the techniques we just discussed.

Know Your Competition

7.1

Know Your Competition

This exercise is designed to assist you in applying some of the techniques for gathering competitive information. Of course, all may not apply. Start by focusing on just one competitor for each technique you use. The important thing at this point is that you try the techniques, get comfortable using them and get results.

Product and service publications

Competitor (optional):	

Key information about products and services:	**Consider the following criteria:**
	What unique products or services does this competitor offer?
	What advantages do their products and services offer over yours and vice versa?
	How do the publications/marketing materials offered by this competitor compare to your materials?

Other comments / observations:

Know Your Competition

Exercise

7.1

Know Your Competition

Customer solicitation

Competitor (optional):	

Information from customers:

Review the following options to determine which are suitable to investigate your competition:

Search Internet

Creative offerings

Talk to your customers

Other comments / observations:

Know Your Competition

Know Your Competition

7.1

"Shopping" the competition

Competitor (optional):	

Information from shopping the competition:	**Observe the following:**
	What unique qualities do customer service and sales people possess?
	Was anything done / offered that surprised you?
	What does your competitor do better than you?
	What do you do better than your competitor?
	How would rate the quality of service (responsive, friendly, knowledgeable etc.)
Other comments / observations:	

Independent evaluations

Competitor (optional):	

Information from independent evaluations:	**Can you use any of the following:**
	Consumer reports
	Internet research
	Better Business Bureau / Board of Trade
	Industry journals and trade magazines
	Competitive research
Other comments / observations:	

Know Your Competition

So what do you do with the information you've gathered? How about creating a report card that can be used to constantly evaluate your business against the competition? Few companies will go to this extent to identify improvement opportunities. Do it and you'll stand out amongst your competition.

Your Competitive Report Card

The challenge in gathering competitive data is that it is constantly changing. Your competitors will find ways to improve or expand their products and services. Your competition itself will expand. Now thanks to the Internet people can shop around the world in just a few clicks! Producing a competitive report card is not a one time exercise. It should be an ongoing evaluation of your market that gets better and more refined as time goes on.

Here's an example: *Clanton and Associates, a mid-sized Architect/Engineering firm specializing in business office development, established a set of customer satisfaction indicators that they tracked on a regular basis. They wanted to:*

- *provide clients with reliable, defect-free products*
- *offer clients project bids that were cost competitive*
- *deliver projects on time and within scope*
- *provide accessible, friendly, prompt, and knowledgeable ongoing support*
- *provide award winning, distinctive building designs for their clients*

They also determined that within the area where they concentrated their sales and marketing, they had at least six competitors. Since much of their work was awarded based on public proposals posted by clients, information on competition was fairly easy to obtain.

Clanton and Associates maintained the following competitive report card:

Know Your Competition

Note: Clanton and Associates is "A" in the chart below.

Competition Indicators	Engineering Firms						
	A	B	C	D	E	F	G
Reliable defect-free products	2	3	1	2	1	3	2
Cost competitive	3	1	3	2	1	1	1
Deliver projects on time/within scope	2	2	2	2	2	3	1
Accessible, friendly, prompt and knowledgeable ongoing support	1	3	1	2	2	3	2
Award winning, distinctive building designs (Total)	1	2	1	2	2	3	1
Number of bids won YTD	4	9	2	4	0	6	2
Revenue growth (Year)	7%	11%	5%	9%	11%	21%	8%

Ratings: 3 = above average   2= average and 1 = below average

Using many of the methods described earlier, Clanton and Associates was able to accumulate information over the years on each of its competitors. Not only did this report card provide a regular yardstick by which to gauge the competition, it actually brought competition together. After comparing competitive data, executive management approached Wellington Steel (F) about merging their companies since their strengths and weaknesses complemented one another!

If you attempt this exercise your initial report card results will be limited and you're likely to question the reliability of the information. **Stick with it!!** As you accumulate more history and pay more attention to your competition, your information will get better and better.

You will find an exercise at the end of this section, should you wish to create your own competitive report card.

To summarize, constantly improving your customer service is critical to the success of your business. But without assessing the service of your competition, how will you know if what you're delivering is really leading edge? Competitive information will drive your business to constantly improve itself. It will force you to avoid stagnating. Make your business stand out by beating your competition at their own game!

Know Your Competition

Your Competition Report Card

This exercise combines the satifactors you identified in Be the Customer and the techniques from Know Your Competition to create a single report card for studying the competition! It is intended to help you compare your business to your competitors on key areas or "satisfactors" you've deemed as important to your customers.

Instructions:

1 Review the satisfactors (sample A) you identified in the Be the Customer exercise. Note: If you wish to change your satisfactors, now would be a good time to do so.

2 Fill in the legend (table 1) with the list of your competitors. Note: six competitors or less is adequate.

3 Fill in the Competition Indicators (table 2) along the left hand column (review sample B for ideas).

4 Fill in the cells (table 2) for each competitor as you gather information. Update this table regularly as more information is gathered or changes occur.

Sample A – sample Competition Report Card

Competition Indicators	Engineering Firms						
	A	B	C	D	E	F	G
Reliable defect-free products	2	3	1	2	1	3	2
Cost competitive	3	1	3	2	1	1	1
Deliver projects on time and within scope	2	2	2	2	2	3	1
Accessible, friendly, prompt and knowledgeable ongoing support	1	3	1	2	2	3	2
Award winning, distinctive building designs (Total)	1	2	1	2	1	3	1
Number of bids won YTD	4	9	2	4	0	6	2
Revenue growth (Year)	7%	11%	5%	9%	11%	21%	8%

Ratings: 3 = above average   2= average   and 1 = below average

Know Your Competition

Table 1 – List your targeted competitors

A	
B	
C	
D	
E	
F	
G	

Table 2 – Competition Report Card

Competition Indicators These are the satisfactors you identified in the **Be the Customer** exercise	Competitors						
	A	B	C	D	E	F	G
Total score per competitor (add column)							

Use this rating scale where applicable:
Ratings: 3 = above average   2 = average and 1 = below average

Know Your Competition

If you completed this exercise you are on your way to knowing your competition. You are one step closer to having the information you need to enhance and align your systems.

Up next, **Learning from the Customer.**

"Optimism is the faith that leads to achievement"
Helen Keller

Learning from the Customer

Chapter 8

Characteristics of Successful Customer-Focused Organizations:

"Aligned their processes and procedures to ensure a quality customer experience."

Now that you have gathered feedback from your customers and evaluated your competition's strengths and weaknesses you can begin to align your processes and procedures with a greater customer focus. To do this effectively you need to be able to trace the flow of the customer through your organization in an efficient and effective way, thus ensuring that the changes you make have the greatest impact on the customer experience. So before we present you with an approach to making changes, let's first discuss two essential concepts used by many highly customer-focused organizations:

1. Moments of Truth

2. Critical Customer Incidents

This chapter:

- provides a definition of Moments of Truth
- offers tips for identifying Moments of Truth
- provides a definition for identifying critical customer incidents
- offers tips and techniques for investigating critical customer incidents
- suggests ways critical customer incidents can be used to aligned your processes and procedures to ensure a quality customer experience. .

Why is this important?

If a company fails to identify its Moments of Truth or fails to recognize critical customer incidents it misses the opportunity to leverage what they know about their customers and competition in order to improve the quality of its service in a strategic way.

Learning from the Customer

Moments of Truth

In 1981, Scandinavian Airlines System (SAS) reported an $8 million loss. The president resigned. The board of directors promoted 39 year-old Jan Carlzon to the position of president. What followed was one of the most remarkable business turnarounds in modern history. In less than two years, Carlzon parlayed that negative $8 million figure into a gross profit of $71 million on sales of $2 billion. To put this into context, the rest of the airline industry was losing an aggregate of $1.7 billion per year at the same time.

> **Moments of Truth**
>
> "A moment of truth is an episode in which a customer comes into contact with any aspect of the company, however remote, and thereby has an opportunity to form an impression."
>
> - Jan Carlzon

Carlzon's simple, effective plan was to actively manage every SAS customer's experience. He reasoned that SAS had 10 million passengers per year and that the average passenger came into contact with five SAS employees. Carlzon believed that his job was to manage those 50 million customer contacts. He called them "moments of truth": 50 million unique, never-to-be-repeated opportunities for SAS to distinguish itself favorably from the competition.

The secret, he believed, was to pay attention to what the customer was conveying with his/her behavior. Every employee was to focus on the customer instead of his/her routine, internally-required duties. Carlzon's goal was to ensure that SAS was selling what the customer wanted to buy. He shifted the mind-set of the company.

Carlzon did not focus on new airplanes and expanded schedules. Instead, he painted planes, spruced up their interiors, intensified customer-service training at all levels of the company and bought more de-icing trucks to ensure on-time departures. Every decision was made with the customer's experience in mind. Each decision was viewed as another opportunity to make a favorable impression.

With astonishing success, Carlzon quickly re-focused an organization of 1,750 middle managers and 3,000 supervisors. His "moments of truth" philosophy, unyielding follow-through, creative mind and ability to clearly and dramatically communicate his expectations, were the mortar and bricks with which he rebuilt SAS. Supporting the mortar and bricks was a solid foundation built on thousands of customer-contact employees whose actions and conscious decisions to make a difference allowed the new structure to stand.

Service quality is the outcome of your moments of truth.

Learning from the Customer

Using Moments of Truth to Enhance Service Delivery

Moments of Truth (MOT) are neither positive nor negative. They simply exist. Service quality is measured by the outcomes of these moments of truth. You may recall in Chapter 1 we showed you a service bell curve.

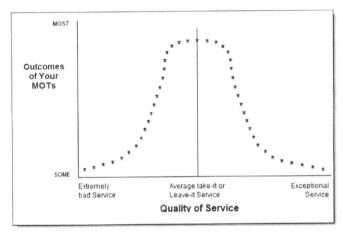

The bell curve shown to the right is a slight variation on that one. This bell curve depicts the outcomes of Moments of Truth in most non-customer focused organizations. As you can see, the outcomes of the vast majority of MOTs are average take-it or leave-it service.

The outcomes of some MOTs include both extremely good and extremely bad service. Two of these are bad.

Obviously extremely bad service loses customers. But so can average service. The only type of service that will contribute to the creation of customer loyalty and return business is service which falls on the right side of the median. Research also confirms that the delivery of consistently high levels of service or exceptional service will create differentiation and long-term loyalty. That means that the service you deliver must be designed to impress your customers.

To ensure that the outcomes of your MOTs are designed to impress the customer, you must first trace the flow of the customer (Cycle of Service) through your business and/or Department looking for touchpoints which will significantly impact the customer's perception.

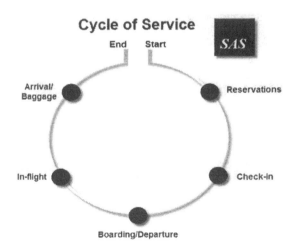

Carlzon focused on the five MOTs shown here. He gathered together all those involved in the success of each moment of truth and then determined what was currently happening, what customers wanted, what would satisfy them and what would impress them. He then established standards of performance which would ensure success at each moment of truth and made certain everyone knew exactly what they needed to do to succeed.

Action

Once you have traced the flow of your customers through your company or department, you can identify your Moments of Truth. Then identify which employees or departments, however remote, are involved in the outcome of each MOT. With input from all those involved, including customer survey data, you can then determine what actions need to be performed which, at the very least, satisfy your customers. But don't stop there. You next need to identify what actions will impress the customer, because impressing the customer is what you must do to create loyalty.

Learning from the Customer

Assign responsibility for the success of each MOT to all those involved and measure each individual's performance against the outcomes of the MOTs. Your employees will now have a clear understanding of what they need to do and you can now hold them accountable for the end results.

Here's an excercise to help you to get started at identifying your MOTs.

Exercise

8.1

Identifying Your Moments of Truth

Using the blank Cycle of Service diagram provided below, trace the flow of the customer through your Company or Department and identify your Moments of Truth.

Cycle of Service

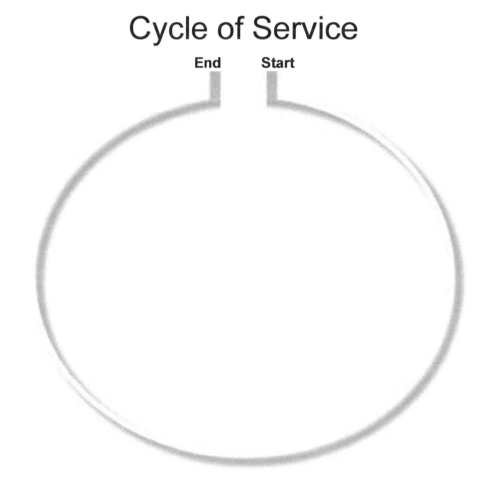

End   **Start**

After you have completed this chapter, schedule a meeting with your staff and identify the Moments of Truth you wish to work on. Then, with this team, determine what needs to be done in order to satisfy your customers' expectations. Brainstorm what you will need to do in order to exceed these expectations at every opportunity.

Learning from the Customer

What are Critical Customer Incidents?

By completing the process in the previous exercise you will be able to integrate strategies for dealing with your predictable MOTs to ensure that the outcomes are customer-focused. But what about the unpredictable? Unpredictability is part of the human condition. Dealing with unpredictability is a critical customer-focused skill. Unpredictable MOTs are events which result in extreme outcomes: extremely impressed or extremely dissatisfied customers. We refer to these as Critical Customer Incidents.

Critical Customer Incidents are extreme events, both positive and negative, that have a significant impact on the way a business conducts itself. Critical Incidents usually lead to the establishment of new policies and procedures or the redefinition of existing ones. They can be used to identify training needs, to uncover improvement opportunities or to expose areas where a business is at risk.

The following are based on real events in two small businesses.

It's 5:30pm. John, a customer support specialist at CompuSource, a small computer networking firm receives an urgent call from the president of a nearby brokerage firm. Their client server network has crashed which will have a financially devastating impact on their service tomorrow morning since the firm is introducing an IPO to its clientele.

John was about to leave for the day but the president sounds frantic. Rather than defer the president until tomorrow (or to a competitor) John places a series of calls to CompuSource's hardware supplier. They have a server but John will need to drive there to get it – about two hours away.

Before doing so he calls his manager who calls the brokerage firm to see if he can retrieve the server files while John drives to pick up the necessary hardware. John and his manager work throughout the evening to restore the client server network. By morning all is up and running.

The president of the brokerage firm is so pleased he awards all future network maintenance and upgrades to CompuSource. John and his manager review the event and decide to market an emergency networking service to all their clients.

This was a **critical customer incident**.

Peter works at the paint counter of a home improvement center. One of his responsibilities is to mix custom colors for customers. A woman requests four gallons of "periwinkle blue". Peter mixes each gallon and loads the four cans into her shopping cart. An hour later the woman returns very upset because the cans tipped over in the back seat of her car while she was driving and one of the lids came off splattering her back seat in paint.

Peter's supervisor explains that the store is not responsible for the spill since they did not load the cans. The woman makes a big scene and threatens to "sue" the store.

This was a **critical customer incident.**

Extreme experiences can be great teachers. Whether they're good or bad they stick in our customer's minds and can be the motivation to change their behavior and their thinking.

Learning from the Customer

A Tail of Customer Service

No it's not a typo – we mean a "tail" of customer service. If you will recall from an earlier chapter, we showed you the bell curve for customer service. To recap, most companies provide mediocre or average customer service. A few provide consistently poor service (negative tail) while a few elite companies provide stellar service (positive tail).

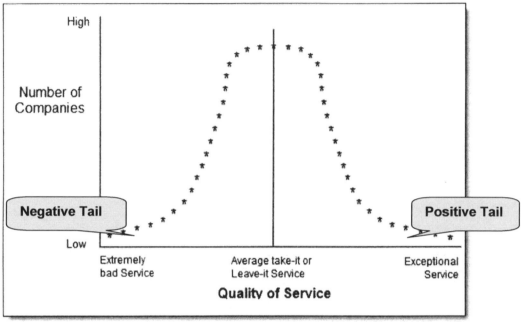

Think of critical customer incidents as events that fall under the negative or positive tails of the bell curve. They are not the typical interactions of everyday business. They are the especially negative or especially positive events that customers remember.

In the chapter, Know Your Customer, hopefully you completed the Be the Customer exercise. The exercise asked you to recall especially good and bad customer service experiences. In essence you were recalling critical customer incidents for those companies - critical from *your* perspective. Whether or not those companies were aware of, or acted on these critical events is the point of this section.

What are some possible indicators of critical customer incidents?

- Service well beyond a customer's expectation or the typical service of your competitors
- Service well below a customer's expectation or the typical service of your competitors
- Extraordinary praise and recognition from customers
- Emotional tirades and outbursts by customers
- Lawsuits waged by customers
- Events referred to as best practices or examples of "how-to" when training staff
- Events that precipitate disciplinary action

The exercise on the following page is designed to assist you in identifying critical customer incidents within your business.

Learning from the Customer

Exercise

8.2

Learning from the Customer

This exercise is designed to assist you in documenting Critical Customer Incidents (CCI) so they can be used to improve your business. You can use this exercise to document a CCI every time one occurs. That way you can build a library of significant events that shape the way you do business.

Note: These can also be used for performance management. When documenting a positive CCI use it to recognize and reward employees involved. If a CCI is negative this documentation could be used to support any disciplinary action initiated with an employee.

Description

Brief title of CCI: **Date CCI occurred:**

Detailed description of CCI:

Indicators of CCI: (check all the appropriate indicators):
- ☐ Service well beyond a customer's expectation
- ☐ Service well below a customer's expectation
- ☐ Extraordinary praise and recognition from customers
- ☐ Emotional tirades and outbursts by customers
- ☐ Lawsuits waged by customers
- ☐ Events referred to as best practices
- ☐ Examples of how-to when training staff
- ☐ Events that precipitate disciplinary action
- ☐ Other (describe)

Employee(s) involved:

Follow up to CCI

If negative, CCI follow-up may include review of existing policies and procedures or development of new one's, additional staff training and/or communications, direct follow-up with customer, disciplinary action etc.

If positive CCI follow up may include review of existing policies and procedures or development of new one's, additional staff training and/or communications, business plan to leverage CCI, reward and recognition, etc.

Recognizing a critical customer incident is important; but how do you learn from it? Next we'll provide some simple pointers on investigating critical incidents and learning from them.

Learning from the Customer

Investigating a Critical Customer Incident

Case study: *Darryl is the manager of a computer development group for a large restaurant franchise. His team develops applications for the company's Intranet that the restaurant managers use to schedule deliveries, maintain staff schedules, submit weekly reports to the corporate office, etc. Based on a complaint from a restaurant manager, he asked one of his developers to rearrange the screen for the staffing scheduler. The changes are minor and basically cosmetic. However, the developer notices a field called Comp Time. Since the company did away with the policy of awarding "comp time" (time off for extra hours by salaried employees) he decides it is no longer necessary. Darryl agrees and tells him to remove the field.*

Big mistake. What Darryl doesn't realize is that several restaurant managers use the field to track excess hours so they can determine if additional staff is needed and as a "burnout indicator".

Darryl receives a litany of calls from many very upset restaurant managers demanding they return the field to the scheduler. Darryl's boss receives several calls as well.

Eventually they were able to correct the scheduler form. This proved to be very costly both in terms of the time it took to correct the problem and the damage to his and his department's reputation.

Since the managers of the restaurants were customers of Darryl and his team, this could be categorized as a Critical Customer Incident. It certainly displayed indicators of a negative CCI: significant detrimental impact on customers and multiple and/or major complaints by customers.

How did it happen? A seemingly minor, innocuous change snowballed into an avalanche of customer complaints. Darryl's manager wanted him to investigate the problem then recommend a process to ensure it wouldn't happen again.

Here are some tips for investigating Critical Customer Incidents

1. Determine the specific event that precipitated the customer impact

Ask: What did we do that caused a problem for our customer?
In the example above it would be easy to assume the problem was the fact that the Comp Time field was removed from the computer application; but really that's just a symptom. The real underlying problem is that there was no procedure to validate the system change with managers (customers) before it was made.

2. Examine your current process

Ask: What is the collective understanding of our policies and procedures related to this problem?
Always begin by examining your current policies and procedures. When investigating a negative CCI solicit input from employees on their understanding of your policies and procedures. If there is wide disparity, then there is no clear process. If one or two individuals misunderstand your process, then you have a training problem.

Learning from the Customer

3. Determine the root causes

Ask: Where did our policy or procedure breakdown?

Continuing with the above example, the cause was that there was no clear process for validating changes with managers. If Darryl wanted to remove the field, there should have been a process by which the change could be run by managers (customers) and approved. Darryl also realized there was no training for his staff. It was *assumed* everyone understood how changes were to be made.

4. Determine follow-up

Ask: What could have been done to avoid this problem? or

What needs to change to avoid this problem in the future?

Once you've pinpointed where your policies and procedures broke down then corrective action should be obvious. If your process is unclear, document the way the process should work. (Be sure to include input from your staff.) If the process is clear but practiced inconsistently among employees, then provide training. In any event be sure training for new employees is updated to include this CCI.

As with any CCI, a good manager must examine how he or she may have contributed to the problem. Perhaps the manager was too lax in providing training. Maybe policies and procedures were not clearly or consistently communicated. When a manager openly accepts a portion of the "blame" he or she communicates a powerful message to employees: It's okay to make a mistake if you own it and take action to correct it.

To summarize

While the above example uses a negative CCI, the process for learning from a CCI is the same whether it's negative or positive. To recap:

Investigating Critical Customer Incidents

Step	Positive CCI	Negative CCI
1. Determine the specific event that precipitated the customer impact	What did we do specifically that had such a positive impact on the customer?	What did we do specifically that had such a negative impact on the customer?
2. Examine your current process	What is our collective understanding of our current process as it relates to this customer issue?	What is our collective understanding of our current process as it relates to this customer issue?
3. Determine the root causes	Where did our actions differ from our current understanding of the process? What did we do differently?	Where did our actions differ from our current understanding of the process? What did we do differently?
4. Determine Follow-up	How can we ensure this successful process becomes part of our regular process?	How can we ensure this problem is avoided in the future?

Learning from the Customer

So you've documented a critical incident and you've extracted that valuable nugget of information it was hiding. Now how do you use the information? The next section tells you how.

Learning from Critical Customer Incidents

The concept is fairly obvious. You learn from your mistakes and your successes. Where companies miss the mark is in leveraging a CCI to improve their business. Here's how to use them:

Interviewing

When interviewing a potential employee describe a negative CCI that occurred at your business. Ask them, "How would you have handled this situation?" or "How do you think this situation could have been handled better?" This will give you some insight into their understanding of the job and their sensitivity to customer service.

Orientation

Negative and positive CCIs are extremely useful in training new employees. Simply telling a new employee, "Customer service is critical," is not good enough. Give them specific examples of what good and bad service looks like.

Performance Evaluations

If an employee is involved in a positive CCI certainly recognize the accomplishment in his or her performance evaluation. If he or she is involved in a negative CCI, determine his or her portion of responsibility and use it as a learning opportunity. Avoid basing an employee's performance evaluation entirely on just CCIs. Overall performance and performance trends are more critical when evaluating employee performance.

Quality Improvement

Good or bad, CCIs can be used to instigate improvement in your business.

Establishing "Best Practices"

If something works, then by all means proliferate it all over your business wherever possible.

Learning from the Customer

Continuous Improvement: Hitting a Home Run

Companies that have suffered significant reductions in market share within the last decade share some common failings. Most have operated under the false assumption that what made them successful in the past will continue to make them successful in the future. Yet, the reality is that tomorrow is certain to be different from yesterday. This reality has created a climate in which companies interested in providing excellent customer service are forced to focus on continuous improvement. In today's market, a company not engaged in ongoing improvement will be perceived by customers as a company on the decline.

> **Rapid, continuous enhancement and alignment of systems and processes which are customer-focused is no longer an option—it is a necessity for survival. Failure to involve every employee in the redefinition of every product and service, failure to invite service innovations on a regular basis from every employee, is folly.**

Most continuous improvement efforts fail simply because most companies are unable to sustain their well-intentioned efforts over time. Too often, management will expound on the importance of a newly-written policy and require employees to take part in special training, only to have it all fall by the wayside. As a result, many improvement efforts are negatively perceived by employees as "just another program." In short, many efforts hardly get beyond the starting point due to a lack of management commitment. Unless management plays a strong and visible role, the hard work involved in changing a company's business practices will not be carried out. Adjusting to any corporate change is difficult for employees—even threatening. It is far easier for them to make excuses for why new policies cannot effectively be carried out.

Continuous service improvement is the core value of a successful organization. Therefore, any successful improvement effort must be a program with no beginning and no end. If employees perceive a beginning and an end to your programs, many will simply wait them out. Anticipating an end, they will adopt a "this, too, shall pass" mentality. When employees are allowed to maintain this mind-set, mediocrity will result.

Not all customers value every service improvement or innovation a company makes. In fact, out of 100 improvements, one customer might value only 10. Another customer might also value 10, although he/she could value 10 different improvements.

Every employee must keep in mind that it is the customer's experience with these innovations that makes the experience special. As a result, it is each employee's responsibility to create a unique, customized experience for every customer.

The manager's role is to get every employee up to bat, to develop and implement new ideas that will improve present performance levels. It's a numbers game; it's a function of "at bats." The more times you come to bat, the more chances you have to get a hit. Still, every improvement idea or attempt at service innovation will not be a home run for the customer. Some may be triples, some doubles and many nothing more than bunt singles. Some ideas will even be strike-outs. One thing is certain, though: if you don't get up to bat, a home run is impossible. Batter up!

Learning from the Customer

To summarize, identifying your Moments of Truth and Critical Customer Incidents is an important opportunity no company can afford to miss. When improvements are required in your systems and processes, ensure that the changes you make are:

- Beyond your customers' expectations

- Valued by the customer (from his or her point of view)

Your objective is to align your processes and procedures to ensure a high quality customer experience.

Use the exercises in this section every time you come across a critical customer incident. You'll find these invaluable nuggets of knowledge in your crusade to win *Customers Forever!!*

Training and Selection

Chapter 9

Characteristics of Successful Customer-Focused Organizations:

"Trained managers, supervisors and employees to reinforce service behaviors."

In your travels as a customer you've no doubt experienced good and bad customer service. Those good experiences include employees who solve your problem quickly and to your satisfaction. It's when someone takes the time to patiently explain your options or how to use a product. It's when an employee recommends an alternative that saves you money. But before employees can provide excellent customer service they have to understand and practice the fundamentals. While it seems new employees or individuals new to the work force would need to practice those fundamentals the most, don't assume your veteran staff have mastered them.

Ensuring that you have the right staff to take on customer service responsibilities and ensuring that all your staff are properly trained is critical if you are to create the customer focus you need.

This chapter:

- describes the attributes of exceptional service providers
- provides a method for evaluating current employee customer-focused behavior and attitudes
- describes what training is needed to be truly customer-focused
- provides tips on hiring/selecting customer-focused employees

Why is this important?

It's easy to assume your employees are providing good customer service; after all, how hard can it be? If the customer needs help, you help them. If the customer has a problem, you fix it, right? But, providing excellent customer service consistently is very difficult. Employees need to know exactly what's expected of them and what good service looks like. Think about how many businesses you interact with on a daily basis. How many provide truly memorable service? It's hard to think of any isn't it? That's because excellent service takes training, work and dedication.

Training and Selection

What Are the Attributes of an Exceptional Service Provider?

Before you start training or hiring service providers it is important to know what to look for. What kind of employee does it take to deliver service that meets both the customer's expectations and needs? What are the characteristics of a truly service oriented employee?

Home Depot, the mega hardware and home maintenance store, offers its products now in most major cities across North America. The home improvement sector is enormous and highly competitive. In a market seemingly saturated with competition, how has Home Depot achieved a return on equity averaging 26% over the past five years, while sales growth continues to better the industry average? The short answer: Home Depot has distinguished itself with a culture obsessed with customer service. Price-wise, Home Depot seems comparable to the competition. But on service, Home Depot is clearly the industry leader. Walk into any Home Depot and you'll find plentiful sales associates willing to patiently provide expert advice. Checkout is fast and easy. There's no hassle associated with returns. How easy is it? Home Depot sales associates have accepted tools on return from disgruntled customers - tools Home Depot doesn't even carry. Why? To win a customer for life.

Home Depot has earned a distinctive reputation for stunning customer service. Actually, it's the employees of Home Depot that have earned that distinction. When you think of world class customer service at Home Depot, you think about the person who helped you. That person is Home Depot. Below is a job description for a Home Depot Sales Associate. Notice the emphasis on customer focus.

Job Summary: Home Depot Sales Associate

Customer service and interaction with customers are key responsibilities of this position. A sales associate must work effectively with customers and other store associates and provide information about products and/or projects. This position also involves stocking merchandise, using tools and equipment, and maintenance duties (e.g., sweeping aisles, down-stocking shelves, etc.).

Presenting a consistent, pleasant, and service-oriented image to customers

Listening and asking appropriate questions to assist customers in completing projects

Assisting and working with other store associates in order to complete job tasks

Using computers, phones, and other equipment

Cleaning and maintaining shelves, end caps, and aisles

Customer Focus: Ability to maintain a positive customer service orientation when dealing with customers on the phone and in person

Stress Tolerance: Ability to work effectively under stressful work conditions (e.g., dealing with multiple customers who need help quickly)

Team Work: Ability to work well with others to achieve common goals

Listening/Communicating: Ability to listen attentively to others, ask appropriate questions, and speak in a clear and understandable manner

18 years or older

Pass a drug test

Be able to work a flexible schedule including weekends, evenings, and holidays

Pass a sales associate test

Pay Information
All jobs are critical to The Home Depot. Based on the competitive retail market, merchandising jobs generally pay more than operational jobs.

Training and Selection

Consider the service providers in your company - the people dealing directly with your internal or external customers. Chances are these people possess the following characteristics:

- Service Mind-set
- People oriented
- Product or service knowledge
- Respect toward customers
- Customer framework
- Effective communicator

Let's explore each of these characteristics a bit more.

Service Mind-set	Throughout this book we have been describing the service mind-set. Exceptional service providers understand the critical importance service plays in organizational success. They intrinsically know that no one is more important than the customer. They recognize that simply satisfying the customer is not enough and go out of their way to exceed their customers' expectations.
People oriented	Employees who are people oriented are more extroverted than introverted. They enjoy and seek out opportunities to work on teams and to interface directly with customers. They create a warm, inviting atmosphere before the customer even speaks to them. They make eye contact, acknowledge the customer and smile. Their non-verbal behavior suggests they are comfortable and enjoy customer interaction. Their enthusiasm is obvious and genuine.
Product or service knowledge	Your best service employees know your products and services inside and out. When they offer the customer options and alternatives, they sound credible and convincing. Now the customer can comfortably make a decision when doing business with your company.
Respect towards customers	Have you ever spoken with a service associate who obviously had more important things to do than assist you, *their* customer? You know the ones that answer you as they walk away, or don't bother to lift their eyes from their work. The ones with a sarcastic tone because you can't find something. The ones who had a bad day so figure it's okay to take it out on you. It all boils down to the person's attitude. They need to believe they are there to service each customer's personal need. The customer and their questions are not a burden. They should be enthusiastically welcomed.
Customer framework	When your best customer-contact employees speak with a customer they do so with a predetermined mental framework for understanding customer needs and offering solutions. They know how to zero in on the customer's need or issue, they offer options, they know what to say and what not to say. They know what phrases to listen for. They educate the customer because an educated customer is likely to be a loyal customer. They know when to escalate issues and when to refer the customer to another person.
Effective communicator	Individuals who provide the best service are those with effective communication skills. First and foremost, listening. They can listen objectively and empathetically to an irate customer. They listen patiently to the indecisive customer and zero in on the customer's key motivations and concerns so they can assist them with a comfortable decision. They speak clearly and in words easily understood by the customer. They avoid phrases that turn customers off. They communicate in a manner which wins customers over.

Training and Selection

Assessing Current Employee Customer-Focused Attributes

Typically, before we begin any training programs with clients, we first undertake a customer-focused training needs assessment. By assessing current employee perceptions of service and interactions with internal partners, you can more effectively determine where to best target the training you need to provide.

You can see an example of one of these assessments on our website.

You can also conduct a less detailed assessment on your own. On the following page is an example of an assessment that you use to get an indication of the current Customer-Focused "climate" in your company.

You may also want to assess current customer-focused skills levels. In the next chapter we will be presenting a framework for interacting with customers and we have included an evaluation tool for assessing your customer-contact employees based on this framework.

Training and Selection

Customer Focus Climate Survey

Please take a few minutes to complete this survey which represents an important step in our journey to service excellence. We value your input and urge you to respond honestly and frankly.

This survey is confidential. You do not need to identify yourself; however, we would like you to indicate your department as we will be using the data collected to obtain an overview of the current customer-focused climate.

Department:
_____
Thank you in advance for completing this survey.

The data gathered from this survey will be incorporated into customer focus training which is planned for later this year.

When considering your responses please think of service in the context of serving customers of the company (external customers) and co-workers, other departments and divisions (internal partners/customers.)

We would like to get your perceptions of service from three different perspectives:

☐ The Organization

☐ The Individual

☐ The Department

Indicate to what extent you agree or disagree with the statements provided by circling the number in the box which best reflects your current opinion. Please respond to all the statements.

As an Organization:

	STONGLY DISAGREE					STONGLY AGREE
1. Service quality is treated as an organizational priority.	1	2	3	4	5	6
2. Our Company has specific service quality standards.	1	2	3	4	5	6
3. Our employees are committed to providing the best level of service to our external customers.	1	2	3	4	5	6
4. Our employees are committed to providing the best level of service to our internal partners/customers.	1	2	3	4	5	6
5. Our employees are encouraged and supported to make decisions and show initiative	1	2	3	4	5	6
6. Our employees are provided with the training needed to provide our customers which exceptional service.	1	2	3	4	5	6
7. Service excellence is recognized and rewarded.	1	2	3	4	5	6

8. One area where we can improve our customer focus and service quality would be:

_____

_____

_____

Training and Selection

As an Individual:

		STONGLY DISAGREE					STONGLY AGREE
9.	I consider service quality to be a priority.	1	2	3	4	5	6
10.	I am encouraged to offer opinions and ideas about improving service.	1	2	3	4	5	6
11.	I can make decisions in favor of the customer, where the company's fiscal responsibilities are not compromised, and feel confident that management will support me.	1	2	3	4	5	6
12.	I treat other departments to whom I provide support as if they were my partner/customer.	1	2	3	4	5	6
13.	The quality of the service I deliver is considered an important factor in my performance appraisal.	1	2	3	4	5	6
14.	I could deliver better service if: _____						

My Department:

		STONGLY DISAGREE					STONGLY AGREE
15.	Has specific standards of performance for delivering high quality service to our external customers.	1	2	3	4	5	6
16.	Has specific standards of performance for delivering high quality service to our internal partners/customers.	1	2	3	4	5	6
17.	Is committed to providing the best quality service to our external customers.	1	2	3	4	5	6
18.	Is committed to providing the best quality service to our internal partners/customers.	1	2	3	4	5	6
19.	Delivers what we say we will deliver when we say we are going to deliver it.	1	2	3	4	5	6
20.	When faced with a choice of serving ourselves or serving and supporting other departments, we put other departments first.	1	2	3	4	5	6
21.	Ensures that traditional policies and procedures do not get in the way of providing service to our customers or internal partners.	1	2	3	4	5	6
22.	Treats delivering service to other departments as a top priority.	1	2	3	4	5	6
23.	Resolves mistakes and errors quickly and accurately.	1	2	3	4	5	6
24.	Meets regularly to identify better ways to deliver service to our customers and internal partners.	1	2	3	4	5	6
25.	One area where we can improve our customer focus and service quality would be:						

Training and Selection

Training

If your customer-contact staff possess the attributes we have described, then you are indeed fortunate. If not, then they need to be trained. Furthermore, since customer focus involves everyone in your organization, employees in non-customer-contact roles will also need training. By assessing your current situation you will be able to determine the extent to which training is required. Our experience suggests that it is quite likely that you will need to train your staff to some extent in order to move you closer to your service vision.

You will recall that thus far we have talked about the need to create a shared vision of what service is, why it is important, the strategic importance of service to your business, developing a strong foundation internally, understanding customer expectations, aligning your systems with customer needs and expectations and leading with customer focus. When it comes to service training many companies jump right into developing skills in service techniques, dealing with angry customers, problem solving and customer relationship management. These are all important...

But...

...unless your employees have the right context, shared vision and understanding of the things we have covered thus far in the book, you will not get the mileage or traction you need to create sustained change and customer focus. Before you focus on skills you need to focus on mind-set, creating the service attitude necessary at all levels throughout your organization.

Through training sessions you can:

- Describe your service vision and create dialogue and buy-in to this vision
- Define and discuss your service values and the behavior needed to turn these values into action
- Discuss what service is and is not in your company
- Present your business case for why service is a critical business strategy
- Explore the impact of customer expectations and what each individual needs to know and do with respect to exceeding customer expectations
- Create a framework for building, maintaining and strengthening strong internal partnerships
- Describe the employees' roles in knowing and learning from customers, and enable them to do this
- Describe the employees' roles in identifying Moments of Truth and Critical Customer Incidents and enable them to do this as well as how to align your systems to enhance the customer experience
- Introduce service standards and dialogue about how employees need to perform their jobs in a way which embodies these standards
- Define how employees will be held accountable for the desired performance
- Determine how to use service recovery pro-actively
- Ensure that each employee commits to a plan of action for how he or she will take what is covered in the training and apply it immediately on the job

(127)

Training and Selection

These are the fundamental building blocks you need if you want your employees to be properly aligned and equipped to move you towards your vision. Interestingly, and perhaps not too surprisingly, this is what our Customers Forever training program focuses on.

You also need to ensure that your managers and supervisors are trained to effectively manage and lead their employees. We have already described the knowledge and skills they need. Your training needs to include all the subject matter we covered in Chapter 4 Customer-Focused Leadership, because "Service is a Leadership Issue".

Training and Selection

Selection

While formal training can give you the biggest bang for your buck, this may not be immediately possible. Mind you, if you completed the calculations in Chapter 1, given the potential gains in profitability and expense reductions, finding budget for formal training would certainly be a good investment.

If formal training is not immediately possible you can take the concepts and exercises provided in this book to review with your employees. This will certainly get the ball rolling. We also have a structured activity guide know as **The Customer Focus Companion** which you could use to help you with your training meetings. We'll tell you about that a little later in this chapter.

In any case, you really do need to take action which will focus your employees on what they will need to do in order to create and sustain the customer focus you want in your organization.

In addition to training, here are some other things that you can do.

1. Hire employees with a good customer attitude

2. Provide employees with examples of positive and negative customer-focused mind-sets

3. Be a role model for positive customer attitude, behavior and focus

4. Hold people accountable for both good and poor service

5. Reinforce and reward exceptional customer service performance on the job

6. Structure your employee development using the Service-In-Action Activity Guide

Let's explore each of these in greater detail over the next few pages.

1. Hiring employees with a good customer attitude

Finding employees with a good customer attitude is difficult, especially in industries that typically have high turnover or a high percentage of temporary positions. On the next page is a tool which may help.

Training and Selection

Customer Associate – Selection Worksheet

Note: This instrument should not be used exclusively when selecting candidates for a service position. You should also consider the candidate's skills and experience as they relate to the bona fide requirements of the position.

When selecting someone for a service position there are several things you can do to determine if they're a good fit. Consider the following:

- History of successful employment in service positions
- Ask the candidate to describe especially good/bad service they've encountered
- Ask the candidate to tell you how they would handle certain customer situations

History of successful employment in service positions

The candidate's resume' will tell the story. Has he/she held positions in service previously? If they've worked in service previously, were they recognized in anyway (i.e. rewards, increased responsibilities)? Ask them for examples where they think they went beyond a normal level of customer service.

Comments:

Ask the candidate to describe especially good/bad service he/she has encountered

This is an extremely powerful exercise. Ask the candidate to describe experiences where he/she was the customer and received outstanding customer service. Ask him/her to contrast that with times when he/she received especially bad service. If candidates can't describe or recognize truly exceptional service it will be difficult for them to critique their own service skills.

Comments:

Ask candidates to tell you how they would handle certain customer situations

Provide the candidates with some examples of customer situations and ask them how they'd handle them. For instance:

A customer is obviously upset about the performance of your product. It turns out he did not install or use the product properly which led to the malfunction. The customer is visibly upset and is complaining loudly in front of other customers. What would you do?

Comments:

A customer has been looking at several options for about an hour. The customer is obviously interested in your product but other customers need your assistance. What would you do?

Comments:

Training and Selection

Action

2. Provide employees with examples of positive and negative customer-focused mind-sets

"Mind-set" or "attitude" can be difficult to describe because it's innate, not something tangible like behavior. Here's a way you can talk about customer attitudes with your employees and make it meaningful. Watch for examples of especially good customer service among your employees. Make sure they're *especially* good. You don't want to set a mediocre standard. When you identify an example write down what you observed. Praise the employee involved, then ask him or her to write down *why* they did what they did. For example:

That's the Attitude!!
Customer Appreciation Certificate

Date: 02/01/2007

Manager: John Dukes

Employee: Mary Hotaling

Customer Service Event: We had a customer who was extremely angry because his special order was late. It turned out the customer had completed the order form incorrectly resulting in a delay by the shipping company. Mary did not blame the customer but rather explained the problem and offered to expedite the order herself. She then called the customer at home when the order came in and made arrangements for the order to be delivered so the customer wouldn't have to make another trip. The customer called the district manager and praised Mary for her initiative. Even though the customer was angry and even though it was the customer's mistake, Mary kept her cool and owned the problem herself. She took a bad situation and turned it around. Way to go Mary!

Customer Service Mind-set: I knew the customer was already angry so even though it was his fault I didn't want his shopping experience to be an unpleasant one. I suppose I could have just explained the error and left it at that but I like the challenge of impressing customers. I'm glad he was happy with his purchase and the fact that he called in to compliment me is really flattering.

This simple technique is very effective at:

- Illustrating specific examples of especially good service for all employees
- Reinforcing your customer focus because peer feedback is viewed as very credible and valid
- Motivating employees - everyone likes positive feedback!

Training and Selection

3. Model a positive customer attitude and focus

Nothing will undermine the customer service attitude of your employees faster than the attitude of management. Unless managers are truly customer-focused they can't expect employees to be. Here's an easy way to demonstrate your customer focus and attitude.

Get into the habit of discussing customer impact every time a problem comes up. For instance:

Don't say......	Say this instead......
To your dishwasher: "You need to get these dishes done. The kitchens backing up,"	"You need to get these dishes done. Our customers are waiting for table settings."
To your mechanic: "Clean up this work station."	"Clean up this work station. We want our customers to view the environment as professional and inviting."
To your claims supervisor: "We're getting too many claims returned because of missing information. We need to figure out why."	"Every time a claim is delayed a customer has to wait to get their certification letter and they usually wind up calling the service line. We need to get to the root cause of these errors."
To your computer developer: "Make sure you complete the testing on the new application by Friday."	"We certainly don't want to implement a system that doesn't meet our customers' needs. Be sure you've tested the application thoroughly."
To your teller: "I know it's been a busy week, but hang in there."	"I know we've been busy but keep a positive attitude. Our customers deserve the same fast, friendly service you've always provided."

If you constantly draw reference to customers and the impact an employee's job can have on them, your staff will quickly internalize the same customer-oriented attitude. This is an easy technique to master. With enough practice it will become almost automatic.

4. Hold people accountable for both good and poor service

Do you have clearly defined job descriptions that include discussion of customer service responsibilities? Do you include service performance in employee performance evaluations?

Most people think that "Accountability" is negative. In other words, holding someone accountable means giving negative feedback. Accountability is both positive and negative. Hold your employees accountable for both good service and poor service. To hold someone accountable you need to have a valid form of measurement that employees are aware of and timely action. When you see someone providing excellent service, let them know what they did well and do this as close to the occurrence as possible. By the same token, when someone provides poor or mediocre service, let them know what they did, as well as what they need to do the next time.

Training and Selection

A lack of accountability actually communicates that service is not important. If good service providers see that poor service is tolerated because no action is taken, it won't be long before the good service providers stop going the extra mile for the customer because they will question whether there is any point in doing the extra work.

5. Recognize and reward exceptional customer service performance on the job

Do you promote employees that have especially good service skills? Do you include a discussion of customer mind-set or attitude when training new staff? Are you consistent and do you include everyone equally when it comes to recognition and reward? Does your staff know what they specifically need to do to be successful in order to earn your recognition or win an award?

Here are a few rules of thumb when it comes to recognition and reward:

- Recognize changes in employee behavior
- Reward consistent performance of the desired behavior
- Be fair and consistent
- Don't just recognize or reward the customer-contact person. Also remember to include any internal partners that may have been involved in the success of a particular MOT or CCI.
- Be sure that the rewards you provide are valued by the recipients

6. Structure your employee development using the Customer Focus Companion

During our many training sessions on service and creating customer focus we have discovered that some managers need a little more structure to help them implement the concepts and approaches we cover in the training and as covered in this book. As a result we have created a highly structured resource with detailed instructions on how to conduct 14 meetings with employees in the development of customer focus. It also includes details on how to set-up and lead Customer-Focused Improvement teams, a team problem-solving process, a detailed personal action planning tool and checklists to keep you organized.

Normally it is used after employees have attended our Customers Forever Training and managers have attended our Customer-Focused Leadership training. You may find this helpful. If you would like more information about this activity guide, please contact us. Our contact particulars are at the front and back of this book. We'll be happy to discuss this option with you.

Training and Selection

The initial training you do is only the starting point. Don't assume that just because people are trained they will automatically change their behavior.

It is up to you as a customer-focused leader to facilitate the changes in behavior you want and need.

It is equally important that you have the right employees in the right positions.

If you have provided training to your employees, established realistic standards of service performance, enabled your employees to perform their customer-focused roles and taken the most appropriate action when employee performance is not at the level you require, you will see results. If you have not done these things and are not receiving the kind of performance you want from your staff, than you have only yourself to blame.

Realistic standards of service performance?

Not to worry, we'll be covering that next.

Service Standards

Chapter 10

Characteristics of Successful Customer-Focused Organizations:

"Defined performance standards for staff that illustrated service behavior and expectations."

The story of the experience in the Ice Cream parlor from Chapter 2 is a classic example of standards gone awry. That doesn't mean that some standards of service performance are not important. Properly developed standards, which are effectively managed, will ensure that you create consistency across your organization particularly at predictable Moments of Truth where it counts. Provided you treat these standards as minimum guidelines and enable your employees to deviate from them if it can enhance the customer experience, then you will see a positive response not only from your customers, but also from your staff.

This chapter:

- discusses important considerations when using service standards

- discusses the need for integrating service standards into training and day-to-day performance

- provides examples of specific customer service standards for greeting the customer, transfers, putting callers on hold and problem resolution

- gives examples of how phone messages, voice mail and email can be used to demonstrate customer commitment

- offers recommendations on how to establish service standards

Why is this important?

Employees need to know exactly what's expected of them and what good service looks like. Well defined and highly customer-focused standards provide your employees which clear definitions of the behavior you require and which you consider important. These standards describe what good service in your organization looks like.

Service Standards

The Need for Service Standards

Webster's defines a standard as:

> *Something established for use as a rule or basis of comparison in measuring or judging capacity, quantity, content, extent, value, quality, etc. A level of excellence, attainment, etc. Regarded as a measure of adequacy.*

You set performance standards for all sorts of things: employee hours of work, breaks, dress, dates and times for reports, etc. This is nothing new. These tend to be pretty clear cut and easy to establish. But when it comes to service standards, there are a number of important considerations.

There are two schools of thought when it comes to the use of service standards.

Some service experts believe that clearly defined service performance standards are essential because they describe exactly what's expected of each employee with a clear definition of the behavior you require and which you consider important. Standards provide the means to objectively measure and evaluate employee performance and ensuring consistency in employee performance.

Other service experts believe that enabling employees to think and act based on your service values and permitting them to make decisions in favor of the customer is a better way to enhance the customer experience. They also believe that service standards can be restrictive and tend to be used to police employee performance rather than be used in a manner for which they were intended which is as a guide to ensure service excellence. The ice cream parlor example in Chapter 2 and the "Step 7" example I gave you about my experience at a steak house are clear examples which support this line of thinking.

So who is right? The reality is that both are right. This represents a significant challenge for you. Establishing a set of service performance standards to which everyone is held accountable is essential, provided each employee has the ability to customize the delivery of service to meet the requirements of a specific customer situation.

There are two types of service standards. We have categorized these as Maintenance Standards and Opportunity Standards.

Two Types of Service Standards

Maintenance Standards:	These are standards which impact day-to-day actions involving everyone in the organization such as answering the telephones, transferring calls, using and responding to voice mail and email etc. Maintenance standards do not impress your customers, at least not after the first time a customer experiences them. For example, answering the telephone within 3 rings and identifying yourself by name is a maintenance standard. While using this standard does not impress customers, failure to use it will certainly irritate them.
Opportunity standards:	These are standards where you have an opportunity to impress your customers. Understanding your Moments of Truth and enabling your employees to exceed customers' expectations at these Moments of Truth provides unique, never to be repeated opportunities to impress individual customers. For example, guaranteeing delivery of a product or service by a certain time and then delivering before that time is an opportunity to impress.

Service Standards

With advances in technology we now have the ability to measure virtually anything. Because of this, some managers attempt to standardize everything simply because they can. This can contribute to standards overload. Make certain that the service standards you put in place are important to and valued by your customers. If the service standard serves some other purpose, you need to ask yourself if you really need it.

We will first discuss Maintenance standards which are sometimes referred to as service hygiene.

Maintenance Standards

Have you ever noticed that some companies answer the phone with a standard greeting, handle transfers flawlessly, solve problems effectively, listen then paraphrase your issue? You notice those things when they're consistent. They leave you with a favorable impression of that company. Typically this is because the company has established specific maintenance standards for how these everyday customer interactions are handled.

Below is a list and description of several common service behaviors where service standards are generally required. We will then walk you through some examples of how to arrive at specific maintenance service standards which demonstrate a real commitment to customer service.

What follows are the absolute basics. If your employees don't perform this way you'll never achieve the level of outstanding service your customers expect.

Greeting	How many times have you walked into a business and not been greeted at all? You make a purchase and maybe the cashier says "hello". Studies show that more than 95% of consumers expect a friendly, personable greeting when they patronize a business. Studies also show consumers are more likely to return to a business where they were welcomed than a business where they were not. So what goes into a personable greeting? • Eye contact • Smiling • Enthusiastic voice • Recognition of the person's name (when possible) • Conversation (That's a nice outfit, Isn't it a beautiful day, etc.)
Listening	Customers need to believe they're being heard. If they have anxieties or concerns about your products or service it's up to your employees to put them at ease. Your employees need to do less talking and more listening.
Customer-friendly language	Customer-friendly language is especially important since many interactions with customers may be over the phone where non-verbals are not a factor. Here are examples of customer-friendly language: • I'll stay with you until the problem's solved • I can do that, I will do that • I'd be glad to • Is there anything else I can do for you?

Service Standards

Maintenance Standards

- It's been my pleasure
- I'm glad I could help you
- (Name) I hope you enjoy your purchase (use customer's name)

Customer antagonistic language includes phrases like:

- You'll have to...
- That's not my job
- I can't, I won't
- Call back
- "They" messed up
- You have the wrong department
- What are you talking about?

Owning the customer's problem

Based on a recent Consumer Affairs Survey, one of the most frequent complaints consumers have about service is that when contacting companies for help they get transferred among departments and bounced from person to person. Many companies have a policy whereby the person first contacted by the customer stays with that customer until the problem is solved. Others require employees to stay on the phone when transferring a call so they can introduce the customer and their problem to the other department or person. Look at how employees resolve problems in your business. If you don't have a documented policy and process - draft one. Far too often employees transfer customers or pass their issue to someone else only to find it falls through the cracks. Customer Ownership is a critical value in companies known for their service like Home Depot, Disney and LL Bean.

Return calls and keep commitments

According to the same survey referenced above, more than 70% of consumers mentioned people being trustworthy and reliable as key factors in providing service. At it's most basic level that means keeping promises.

Demonstrate comprehension

Consumers will view your service as higher and more professional if an employee understands their problem or situation even if that employee doesn't solve the problem to their complete satisfaction. So how do employees demonstrate comprehension? They can use a simple technique called *paraphrasing*. Before they offer a solution they say:

"So let me make sure I understand your situation..."

"As I understand it, the problem is....."

Once the problem is understood the employee should then ask the customer what would satisfy them or what would rectify the situation - i.e.; "I understand the problem. What would be the ideal solution for you?" "I'm certainly sorry this happened. How can I help you rectify this?"

After the employee demonstrates he or she understands the problem, he/she can then offer a solution or, even better a choice of solutions.

Service Standards

Maintenance Standards

Memorable good-byes   This sounds like one of those Sunday afternoon tear-jerker movies but it's not. Don't let a customer walk away with a ho-hum experience; make them remember your company. At a minimum an employee should:

- Ask if there's anything else he/she can do for the customer
- Thank the customer for their business
- Invite the customer back
- Ask if there's anything your company could have done to make their experience more pleasant
- Compliment them on their purchase

Developing Maintenance Service Standards

When it comes to establishing standards for the way everyone handles your basic customer interactions such as answering the telephone, transferring calls, dealing with messages, etc. it is important that the customer is left with the impression that the person they are dealing with is genuine and spontaneous. Developing basic scripts **which people can use as a guide** may be a useful technique but please be forewarned. We are not big fans of using scripts because quite often people come off sounding like they are simply reading a script. Customers don't like that. Clearly it is important to ensure that this does not happen. There are however a few times when a consistent script can be helpful in teaching people what you are trying to accomplish. Here's what we mean.

1. Greetings (Telephone)   Surveys show that companies that use a standardized greeting are perceived as more professional and competent than those that do not. It may seem like a small issue but imagine this hypothetical customer call:

Employee:	"Jenkins."
Caller:	"Is this Jenkins Autobody?"
Employee:	"Yes it is."
Caller:	"Is this Roger?"
Employee:	"No, this is the operator. That line's busy. I'll transfer you to the service department. Hold on..."
Caller:	"No, no, I don't need your service department. I'm calling about a problem with my bill."
Employee:	"You want Roger Baxter. You dialed the wrong number."
Caller:	"This is the number that was left on my voice mail."
Employee:	"I'll transfer you."

(139)

Service Standards

A simple call, already off to a bad start. Compare that now to a company using a policy of standardized greetings:

Employee:	"Jaybees Autobody repair, this is Jim Brady, service associate. How can I help you?"
Caller:	"I'm looking for Roger. I have a question about my bill."
Jim Brady:	"That would be Roger Willis in our business office. Who can I say is calling please?"
Caller:	"This is Allen Philips."
Jim Brady:	Can you hold Mr. Philips while I transfer you?"
Caller:	"Sure."

Here are a few things to consider when you establish a standard for answering the telephone.

Action

A standard greeting makes it easier to quickly ascertain the purpose of someone's call. A standardized greeting should include the following:

- Company name
- Department
- Full Name
- Offer of assistance

Action

For proper business etiquette and creating a polished image in the mind of your customer, remember the following:

- Answer the phone within 3 rings.
- Give full attention to the caller .
- Do not eat or chew gum while speaking to a customer.
- Speak clearly.
- Whenever possible use the customer's name.
- Be personable and enthusiastic.

2. Transfers (Telephone)

Believe it or not, there was a school of thought in the 70's that suggested it was okay, and actually better, to transfer a caller without introducing the caller or the caller's issue. The theory was that by having the customer repeat his or her story again and again it would desensitize them to the problem. It wasn't a good idea then and it's a worse idea now when fuses and patience seem to be a lot shorter.

Service Standards

Action

Here are the several important considerations when transferring a caller:

- First, be sure you have to transfer them; it's always best if a caller can be helped without transferring.
- Ask the customer if they can hold while you transfer them (sometimes they can't).
- Explain to the caller if they will hear silence.
- Stay on the line until the party answers.
- Introduce the caller and his/her issue .
- Excuse yourself from the call.

Let's continue the previous example:

Employee:	"Jaybees Autobody repair, this is Jim Brady, service associate. How can I help you?"
Caller:	"I'm looking for Roger. I have a question about my bill."
Jim Brady:	"That would be Roger Willis in our business office. Who can I say is calling please?"
Caller:	"This is Allen Philips."
Jim Brady:	"Can you hold Mr. Philips while I transfer you?"
Caller:	"Sure."
	(transferring)
Roger Willis:	"Roger Willis, Business Office, how can I help you?"
Jim Brady:	"Roger this is Jim. I've got Allen Philips on the line. Can you assist him with a question about his bill?"
Roger Willis:	"Certainly."
Jim Brady:	"Thank you for calling, Mr. Philips"

3. Putting callers on hold	We've all experienced the frustration of being put on hold for what seems to be an eternity. Some companies have a phone system that provides the caller with an estimate of their wait time. Most don't have that sophistication.

Action

If you need to put the caller on hold be sure to follow these guidelines when you establish standards:

- Ask the caller if it's okay to put him or her on hold; if not, ask for a convenient time to call him or her back.
- Apologize for the inconvenience.

Service Standards

- If possible give them an estimate of how long they may be on hold.
- Check back every thirty to sixty seconds so the caller knows you haven't forgotten. (Realize that 30-60 seconds will seem a lot longer to the caller.)

For example:

Roger Willis: "I'll need to pull your file Mr. Philips. Is it okay if I put you on hold or would you prefer a call back?"

Caller: "No, I can wait."

Roger Willis: "I apologize for any inconvenience. This shouldn't take more than a minute or two."

(45 seconds later)

Roger Willis: "Just a minute longer. My secretary is bringing in your file."

Caller: "Thanks."

4. Problem resolution   There's a definite skill in assisting a customer with defining exactly what it is they need. You know your business. You know how your products and services are delivered, implemented, installed, invoiced, put together and how they're paid for. You know what sizes and colors they come in. You know the difference between the 385XT20 and the 456DD32. Customers may sound like they're speaking a foreign language.

 Action

When a customer calls use this simple framework for establishing standards concerning how to quickly ascertain their need:

- Be sure you understand the customer's problem before offering a solution.
- Paraphrase what the customer has said and offer your understanding of the problem. (So what I understand is you need me to...)
- Apologize for any inconvenience.
- Ask the customer what will satisfy the problem. (What would correct this problem to your complete satisfaction?)
- If you can't provide the solution the customer is looking for, apologize, explain why and offer another alternative or choice of alternatives.
- Personally commit to the resolution. (I'll work on this issue myself. Is there a number I can reach you at later?)
- Commit to a timeframe for resolving the issue. (I'll get back to you by the end of today with an answer.)

Research shows that if you are apologetic, empathic and competent and deliver on your commitment, most customers will not only forgive any infraction but will actually walk away with a positive impression of your company! Seems customers expect companies to make mistakes and are more surprised when they correct them to their satisfaction!

Service Standards

Now let's look at what you need to consider when establishing standards for Voice Mail, Phone Messages and E-Mail.

Voice Mail, Phone Messages and Email

Interactions with your customer's won't always be person-to-person. There will be those times when you trade phone messages or emails. Service standards related to how these important functions are handled are critical.

1. Voice mail   Most customers don't like leaving a voice mail message. They want an answer or help as soon as possible.

If a customer gets your voice mail be sure it provides the following:

- Your name and department
- Today's date
- An idea of when you'll return / your availability
- What to do / who to call if it is an emergency

For example: "This is Matt Adams with the Mortgage Lending department. Today is Tuesday, February 16th. I'm in the office but in meetings until 2pm. If you'd like to leave a message please leave your name, number and a detailed message after the tone. If you need immediate assistance please call Steven Perry at 555-4532. Thanks for calling and have great day."

Other things to standardize for managing voicemail include:

- Update message frequently (daily if possible)
- Check for messages frequently (at least three times a day)
- The tone, and clarity of your message
- Who to call in your absence
- When they can expect a return call

2. Phone messages   Actually leaving a phone message is very much like your voice mail greeting except you add the date, time and purpose of your call.

When leaving a customer a message include the following:

- Your name, company and department
- Date and time of your call
- Purpose of your call

Service Standards

- An explanation of your schedule / availability if they want to call back
- How you or someone else can be reached in event of an emergency

3. E-mail   It's the reality of today's business world. More and more business is being conducted over the Internet. It's fast. It's universal. It's easily accessible from anywhere in the world. And, it's here to stay so make it work for you. If you're exchanging emails with a customer do him or her a favor. Make it easy to manage. Assuming your email message is just one of many your customer will be sifting through, by making it especially professional, your service will stand out.

Action

Here's what to consider when establishing email standards:

- Be brief, but specific
- Include your company name / department
- Use an action oriented memo line e.g. MEETING REQUEST, REVIEW PROPOSAL, ISSUE RESOLVED
- Clearly state what action you'd like the customer to take (if any)
- Copy only those necessary
- Include your pager, phone, fax and cell phone number if possible
- Don't use email when a telephone call will resolve the matter more quickly and easily

Action

Here are a few things to keep in mind when managing your own email:.

- Check your email at least three times a day
- Keep your mailing lists updated
- Keep a specific folder for each customer rather than mixing all messages

On the next two pages we have provided you with an example of some service maintenance standards. This should help you to get started at creating your own.

Service Standards

Sample of Basic Customer Service Standards

We will meet and endeavor to exceed the expectations of our customers through exceptional service.

We will demonstrate professionalism and integrity in all our customer interactions and business practices.

We will present ourselves to our customers, clients, vendors, and other third parties as an efficient, customer-focused organization, whether in person, by telephone or in correspondence.

<u>By Telephone:</u>
All telephones will be answered by the third ring.
We will ensure coverage for our telephone when not available to answer it personally. When this occurs we will:

- ensure that a co-worker will answer the telephone in our absence
- forward the telephone to a line which will be answered in our absence
- ensure the person to whom our calls are forwarded is aware of our whereabouts and expected return time
  and/or
- provide contact particulars on our voice mail message together with our expected return time.

The standard telephone greeting will be: "Good morning (afternoon, evening) thank you for calling (Company name and your location/department) this is (state your name), How may I help you?"

The maximum time a caller will be placed on hold is 30 seconds, and when this occurs we will:

- ask permission to place caller on hold
- inform caller of expected wait time (if known)
- offer caller the option of leaving a message, or determine if someone else can be of assistance
- follow-up to ensure caller is not on hold longer than 30 seconds

When directing calls to another telephone we will:

- identify to whom the call is going
- ensure the call is received
- introduce the caller and provide any other information, when known

When taking messages we will:

- ensure the intended person receives the message within 15 minutes of returning to their workstation
- provide full name of caller as well as:
  - return telephone number
  - date and time of call
  - the purpose of the call (when possible)
  - any other relevant information about the caller

Telephone calls will be returned the same day.

We will use the caller's name at least once during the call.

We will thank the caller for calling.

Service Standards

Sample of Basic Customer Service Standards

<u>In Person</u>
We will always place paperwork or other administrative activities aside and give the customer our immediate, undivided attention.

Customers and other visitors will be acknowledged immediately and greeted in a friendly and pleasant manner.

We will use the customer's name at least once during any interaction.

When unable to assist someone, we will identify someone who can be of assistance, introduce the customer to this individual and briefly explain the customer's request

We will wear the appropriate, approved name tag (personal identification) at all times.

<u>Correspondence and Email</u>
We will acknowledge receipt of correspondence and email on the same day as receipt.

This acknowledgement can be by telephone or by email as appropriate.

If unable to respond completely to request at that time, we will provide a timeframe within which a full response will be provided.

All information provided to customers will be complete and accurate.

We will deliver on all promises within the time frames outlined, without exception, both to our customers and each other.

We will respond to all requests within 24 hours.

We will ensure that professionalism, privacy and confidentiality are maintained in all our interactions and communications. We will do this by:
- complying with all Corporate or project dress codes and codes of conduct
- endeavoring to discuss all problems as discreetly as possible to ensure confidentiality
- not discussing customer or company business outside of work
- not openly discussing customer names, situations, etc. within earshot of others
- ensuring that all information conveyed to customers is clear and accurate, specific to their needs, consistent, comprehensive, and provided within the timeframe promised

We will ensure that our work area and premises are maintained in a neat and orderly condition.

When responding to a customer complaint we will:
a) Respond immediately and if possible, deal with it personally.
b) Listen attentively.
c) Ensure the customer is speaking to someone who can help (if unable to deal with the complaint, identify who can, introduce the customer, explain the circumstances).
d) Never argue with the customer, always apologize for the inconvenience and work together on arriving at a reasonable solution.
e) When problems can not be solved immediately, provide a timeframe, outline the steps required, and follow through to ensure this deadline is met.
f) Always ensure complaints are responded to with urgency and dealt with within 24 hours.
g) Maintain contact with the customer until issue is resolved.
h) Ensure a record of the complaint is kept as well as the steps taken to resolve it and forward this to your supervisor.

Service Standards

Opportunity Standards

You will recall in a previous chapter we discussed Moments of Truth. Jan Carlzon had identified 5 primary Moments of Truth. At each of these MOTs he and his employees established opportunity standards based on what they knew their customers expected. For example, at check-in, they focused on wait times (how long the customer had to wait to be served) by ensuring adequate staffing and they focused on the interactions with customers when it came to the enforcement of rules and policies. Employees were given the flexibility to customize the application of these rules based on individual customer circumstances. When it came to departure times, they acquired additional de-icing equipment and ensured that teams were always ready to de-ice planes so they would take-off on time.

As you traced the flow of the customer through your company in the Moments of Truth exercise you identified predictable Moments of Truth. You also determined what would satisfy and impress your customers. It is at these touchpoints that you can establish service opportunity standards.

For example, for a courier company like Federal Express, a key Moment of Truth is when a package gets delivered. An opportunity standard that they have established, with which most of us are familiar, is a guarantee of next day delivery by 10:00 AM.

This is a great opportunity for you to get your employees involved in determining what the minimum standards should be. You will be surprised by what they may come up with.

What is critically important is that the standards established describe the behavior and actions you want people to exhibit. If you use vague language, people may not know exactly what is expected. Your standards need to be something that can be measured or <u>observed</u>. These also need to be viewed as equitable, the same for everyone, and realistic. There is no point in setting a standard that can rarely be attained. This tends to frustrate rather than motivate.

Your standards should also embody your service values and these need to be reinforced through accountability.

All employees need to fully understand why these standards are important, how these standards impact on their jobs, how they will be held accountable, what the consequences are if they do not perform their jobs in accordance with these standards, and how their performance will be recognized and rewarded when they exemplify these standards. Ensure that these issues are addressed in the training you provide to your employees.

Include evaluation of these standards within your performance management system. Remember, if you do not pay attention to their performance with respect to these standards, your employees will not pay attention either. If they are underperforming, coach them, give examples of what good performance looks like. Help them to improve.

Service Standards

CAUTION!!

Remember. If you manage people to comply with your standards, you will get compliance. People will act like robots. They will follow the rules. You want them to buy in, not give in.

When you set your standards do not make them too restrictive. Do not put your employees in a position where they must enforce a standard which may have a negative effect on the customer. If you teach them **why** these standards are important, and you enable them to customize the application of these standards to suit individual customer circumstances, that will go a long way to ensuring you don't encounter a "Step 7" scenario like my experience in the Steak House.

"In my life I've always wanted to be somebody. But I see now
that I should have been more specific."
Christy, In search of Intelligent Life in the Universe

Pro-Active and Effective Service Recovery

Chapter 11

Characteristics of Successful, Customer-Focused Organizations:

"Utilized pro-active service recovery as a means to strengthening customer relationships"

It's going to happen. At some point someone will be unsatisfied with the service or product they received. There's no way around it. But, if you have a plan for fixing those errors, and if you do it quickly and effectively, you'll actually distinguish yourself from your competition.

What does service recovery mean? Sounds like something that takes place in the emergency room doesn't it? Actually that's not far off! Think of service recovery as an emergency room for your customer relationships.

Here's an example of a company that turned what started as a major blunder into an experience that won a customer for life.

> *A woman purchases a new car only to have the car break down a few days later on her way to the airport.*
>
> *She phones the dealership incensed that her new car has broken down and that she has a plane to catch. The service manager apologizes for the inconvenience and arranges for a tow truck to pick up the vehicle. He also phones his secretary to ask if she can pick up the woman on her way to work and take her to the airport. The woman catches her flight.*
>
> *During her business trip, the woman receives a call stating that the car has been fixed and that it will be waiting for her upon her return. The service manager and secretary meet the woman outside the terminal with her car and return to work in another car.*
>
> *A week later the service manager calls the woman and asks if there are any problems. She also receives a letter from the service manager and coupons for two free oil changes. The letter also provides an explanation of the mechanical problem and indicates that the problem has been reported to the manufacturer.*
>
> *The woman, so impressed with the service she receives, vows never to buy a car from another dealer.*

That's recovery.

This chapter:

- explains why service recovery is of strategic importance
- discusses the development of specific, pro-active recovery plans
- provides an analysis tool to help you determine the current state of your service recovery methods
- provides and approach for dealing with angry customers

Why is this important?

When mistakes are made and the customer is unhappy you have an extraordinary opportunity to demonstrate just how much you value his or her business. As we have mentioned already, when you recover from mistakes in a way that impresses customers, you can actually increase their loyalty and win them for life.

Pro-Active and Effective Service Recovery

The Strategic Importance of Recovery

In Chapter 6 we shared some important statistics with you, and these warrant repeating.

When it comes to service, most customers don't complain. There are many reasons for that.

The number one reason is that most customers don't think it will do any good. Other reasons include: customers don't want the hassle, don't know who to complain to and don't want to be forced to jump through hoops when they do have a complaint. It is just easier to take their chances elsewhere.

Think about the times you have wanted to complain about service. If you did actually complain, have any of the following things happened to you?

The person you are complaining to:

Most Customers Don't Complain

- 96% of customers who are dissatisfied with service don't complain.

- 90% of these customers will not come back again.

- Each one will tell a minimum of 9 to as many as 20 other people about his or her experience.

Here's the math. If you receive 1 complaint:

# who don't complain	= 24
# who don't come back	= 22
# of people told about bad experience	= 198

- goes out of their way trying to prove that you are wrong
- tries to prove that what they did was right
- tries to show you that the problem was actually your fault
- tries to show you that it's not their fault
- tries to convince you that it's no one's fault
- takes no responsibility and tries to transfer you to another department

If none of these things has happened to you, count your lucky stars. You're in the minority.

The customer that doesn't complain, but doesn't come back, is the one that hurts your business most of all!

Consider these additional facts:

- About 75% of customers will do business with you again if their problem is handled in a positive way.
- 95% of customers will do business with you again if their problem is handled in a positive way…on the spot.

There is a direct correlation between the time it takes to resolve a complaint and the willingness of a customer to continue dealing with you. There really is no room for failure. If you do not empower your customer-contact staff by providing them with the knowledge, skills and authority to resolve customer complaints on-the-spot, you run the risk of losing customers forever.

Pro-Active and Effective Service Recovery

Recovery – Pop Quiz

1. If a problem occurs with 100 of your customers and the problem is resolved on the spot in a manner which exceeds their expectations, how many would in all likelihood return to do business with you again?

   Answer: _____

2. In the same scenario, given what you know about the number of customers who complain, if you have received 100 complaints how many customers are likely to have experienced the same problem and not complained?

   Answer: _____

3. Based on your answer to question 2, how many customers are not likely to return to do business with you again?

   Answer: _____

4. Out of 2500 of your customers, 100 complained as in question 1 and you fixed the problem immediately to their complete satisfaction, how many customers could you have left.
   Answer: _____

5. Based on your calculations in question 4, at a minimum, how many bad stories would be circulating about the poor service your company provides?

   Answer: _____

Answers:

1. 95% X 100 = 95

2. 96% X 100 = 96

3. 90% X 96 = 86

4. 100 complaints means 2400 didn't complain. (2500 X 96% = 2400) Out of this number 90% (2400 X 90%) equaling 2,160 would not come back. Therefore you would have 335 customers left. (2400 minus 2160 = 240 plus 95% of 100 registered complaints = 240 plus 95 which equals 335)

5. 2,160 non-complaining customers will tell at least 9 others so you would have 19,440 bad stories circulating about your poor service. That's got to hurt.

Get the point?

Pro-Active and Effective Service Recovery

Personal Recovery Strategies

1. DO IT RIGHT THE FIRST TIME

It is essential that all employees strive to do their service job right the first time. You cannot rely on merely recovering in a positive way to gain customer loyalty. Mistakes mean a lack of service quality! If your employees are making a lot of service mistakes, being great at recovery simply means they "mess up" quite a bit. Every employee must attempt to provide excellent service to every customer and rely on recovery only as a secondary service tactic.

This means that you need to find out what your service mistakes are to achieve a "do it right the first time" approach. The best method of getting this information is from customer complaints. They provide you with the necessary feedback to fix repeated service problems. Every employee must keep track of what customers complain about. This information should be talked about within each work group, shift or department, and repeat problem situations should then be corrected.

RULES TO LIVE BY
Place no blame, just solve the problem.
Assume total responsibility for "making it right".
Quickly attempt to correct the problem or let someone who can help know immediately.
Remain concerned and sympathetic.
Remain Helpful (find someone to help if you can.)
Remain apologetic.
Remain Interested.

When mistakes are made, it is rarely the mistake that irritates the customer. In most cases, it is the way the mistake is handled. If your desire to be the best is sincere, then your employees must do everything in their power to keep a positive attitude with every customer.

2. MAKE IT EASY FOR CUSTOMERS TO COMPLAIN

You must make it easy for customers to complain. You need to understand that you are in the best position to know when customers are displeased. You see their reactions, hear their voice tones and listen to their comments. The question is… what do you do when you find a dissatisfied customer...

...quickly attempt to correct the problem or let someone who can help know immediately?

...ignore the situation and do nothing unless the customer directly complains?

Remember, when things go wrong customers are primed for a fight. Normally, when these customers become frustrated or angry, they expect less from the company in the future. If you recover impressively by:

> **A customer that complains is doing you a great service!**

- acknowledging the mistake
- expressing your concern and apologizing
- taking quick action to resolve the problem

...you can greatly exceed the customer's expectations. The mistake made actually creates a unique opportunity to surprise customers with service they will brag about later. Recovery situations provide an opportunity to be magnificent.

Pro-Active and Effective Service Recovery

3. MAKE RECOVERY HASSLE -FREE

The ability to turn service mistakes into memorable service experiences is fundamental to an outstanding service reputation.

Making quick, effective and hassle-free problem-solving a part of the everyday job priorities leaves a positive impression on customers.

> **Remember, it can take months to find a customer and only seconds to lose one!**

Reliable recovery efforts dramatically communicate to customers that your organization cares, that it is sensitive to the customer's needs, and that it will stand behind its product or service—no matter what. Unfortunately, an angry, irritated customer gets treated to a rebuttal more often than they are offered a sympathetic ear! But nothing is ever gained by winning an argument and losing a customer.

A large percentage of your potential customer complaints are predictable. And there is a good chance your employees already know what these are. You already know from your current experience what many of your customers like and don't like. Your customer research can give you even greater information upon which to act. For instance:

> *Let's say your company may be bound by legal compliance regulations regarding the treatment of information, or following a process prescribed by regulators. These processes are necessary and you must comply or face prosecution. The problem is these processes are cumbersome and irritate some customers. As a result, the potential for complaints and customer dissatisfaction is high. You know you need to follow the regulations and that the customer is going to blame you, not the regulator. This creates a great opportunity for predetermining how your employees can handle such situations in a manner which impresses the customer even though you can not change the rules and regulations.*

I suspect that you may have some operational policies and issues that you currently employ which probably irritate your customers. While your first course of action should be to see if that policy or procedure can be changed to be more customer-friendly, if in fact you can't change it, the question becomes what can you do to ensure that, if these complaints occur, your employees handle the situation in a way that at the very least satisfies the customer?

By anticipating all your potential recovery situations and developing pre-determined actions that your employees can take when these situations occur, you will be able to recover on the spot.

Action

A good way to do this is to revisit the Moments of Truth exercises you have done, and determine what can go wrong, or what typically goes wrong at these Moments of Truth. Then, together with your employees, devise specific strategies for how you can turn lemons into lemonade. How you can quickly and effectively resolve the problem. Then empower your employees to fix customer problems by ensuring they know what they can do and how far they can go in dealing with a situation.

In many cases, service is about paying attention to the little things. When it comes to interactions with customers there are things you can say and should not say, do and should not do, as a matter day-to-day customer encounters. Let's take a moment to consider some of these.

Pro-Active and Effective Service Recovery

What to Say... What Not to Say

There are certain phrases and actions, both good and bad, which make customers take notice when dealing with any company.

Here are the phrases:

Phrases to use	Phrases to avoid
Thank you, you're welcome, please, I apologize, excuse me, etc.	I can't help you..., That's not our fault..., It's not our policy
Can I be of assistance? May I help you? etc.	You must be mistaken
We appreciate your business, thank you for shopping with us today, etc.	You should have... You shouldn't have....
Is there anything else I can do for you?	What do you want me to do about it?
It's been a pleasure helping you...	We don't handle that...
Do you have any suggestions for improving our service?	There's nothing I can do...

The bottom line is this...there will be plenty of occasions when a customer has misused your product, not followed instructions, reacted emotionally rather than logically, etc. It is important to avoid the temptation to point that out and defend your business. Do you want to win the argument or win the customer?

What to Do... What Not to Do

Just as you need to be careful about what you say, you have to watch what you do. In fact, your non-verbal behavior can lose customers before you even speak with them.

Non-Verbal behavior to use	Non-Verbal behavior to avoid
Make and maintain eye contact, smile	Adverse facial expressions, rolling eyes
Allow a comfortable distance/space	Talking over your shoulder or as you walk away
Appear and sound enthusiastic	Gesturing to the customer rather than speaking
Maintain a neat, professional appearance	Appearing bored, lethargic

Pro-Active and Effective Service Recovery

Take a few minutes to complete this self-assessment to determine how effective and pro-active your current recovery efforts are.

Exercise

How Effective are Your Recovery Efforts?

Circle the number which represents how much you agree with each statement.

11.1

Recovery Efforts Are Fast and Distinctive	Completely Disagree					Completely Agree
1. Our recovery efforts are customer-friendly.	1	2	3	4	5	6
2. We guarantee customer satisfaction.	1	2	3	4	5	6
3. Employees are empowered to solve customer problems quickly and efficiently.	1	2	3	4	5	6
4. Our customers have easy access to the people they need to talk to.	1	2	3	4	5	6
5. Our recovery efforts are distinctive from that of our competitors.	1	2	3	4	5	6
6. We give the customer the benefit of the doubt.	1	2	3	4	5	6
7. The customer's perception of a problem is considered significant at every level of the organization.	1	2	3	4	5	6
8. Employees are permitted to deviate from planned actions or operating procedures when they see the need.	1	2	3	4	5	6
Sub-Total						

Potentially Dissatisfied Customers Proactively Identified	Completely Disagree					Completely Agree
9. We endeavor to identify dissatisfied customers before they complain.	1	2	3	4	5	6
10. Identifying customer problems is clearly defined as everyone's job.	1	2	3	4	5	6
11. Our employees perceive identifying a problem to be rewarding.	1	2	3	4	5	6
12. Multiple methodologies (surveys, call-backs, comment cards, employee data gathering) are used to identify customer problems.	1	2	3	4	5	6
13. Toll-free lines are available for customers to communicate with someone who has the ability to solve the customer's problem.	1	2	3	4	5	6
14. Access to the company is user-friendly and well communicated to the customer.	1	2	3	4	5	6
15. We act quickly on customer information when it is received.	1	2	3	4	5	6
Sub-Total						

Pro-Active and Effective Service Recovery

Recovery Efforts Are Strategically Planned

	Completely Disagree				Completely Agree	
16. Potential problems are identified as part of process improvement efforts.	1	2	3	4	5	6
17. Plans have been developed to quickly and efficiently deal with common problems (predictable MOTs).	1	2	3	4	5	6
18. These plans and the actions that need to be taken are widely understood.	1	2	3	4	5	6
19. Recovery efforts are perceived to be an essential part of the customer focus process.	1	2	3	4	5	6
Sub-Total						

Systematic Evaluation and Improvement of Process Effectiveness

	Completely Disagree				Completely Agree	
20. The types and frequency of customer problems are tracked systematically.	1	2	3	4	5	6
21. The root causes of problems are identified.	1	2	3	4	5	6
22. This information is used to improve delivery processes well as organizational practices.	1	2	3	4	5	6
23. We routinely evaluate the effectiveness of our recovery efforts from the customer's point of view.	1	2	3	4	5	6
24. Our recovery actions achieved the desired customer effect: i.e., we create a loyal customer.	1	2	3	4	5	6
25. We use the information we learn through our errors and in recovery efforts to improve our process.	1	2	3	4	5	6
26. Our actions send the symbolic message to all employees that we are committed to not just satisfying but, exceeding customer expectations.	1	2	3	4	5	6
Sub-Total						
Total						

Sub-total your responses by adding your ratings together for each section of the assessment. Add your sub-totals together to arrive at your total score. The best possible score is 156.

If your score is between 130 and 156 your recovery efforts are truly strategic and effective. Given the strategic importance of pro-active recovery and the financial impact on your business of less than highly effective recovery, if your score is under 130, you should develop a plan to do whatever is necessary to increase your effectiveness in each of the areas identified in this assessment.

Pro-Active and Effective Service Recovery

Dealing with an Angry Customer

More than likely, when a customer is making a complaint he or she is upset. The following is a simple model to use when dealing with an angry customer.

1. ☑ Listen to the customer
2. ☑ Don't counter with defense or blame
3. ☑ Empathize with the customer's situation
4. ☑ Ask what would satisfy them
5. ☑ Offer the best solution or alternatives
6. ☑ Deliver more than the customer expects
7. ☑ Follow up to ensure satisfaction

1. Listen to the customer

Action

Give the customer an opportunity to vent his or her frustrations. Interrupting the customer before they have said what is on their mind or assuming that you know the cause of the problem and providing an answer before the customer is finished stating their concern, will only add fuel to the fire. Listen for the specific root cause of the customer's discontent. Once the customer has a chance to present their problem, then you can probe for additional information.

2. Don't counter with defense or blame

Action

It's tempting to defend your product or service, particularly if the customer is being especially hostile. Don't assign blame to someone or something. Never put the customer off or tell them that "my department doesn't handle that". The person receiving the complaint must accept responsibility for solving the problem.

Keep in mind that it may sound like a personal attack, but it's the product or service they're unhappy with. If an employee becomes defensive, this behavior will turn the interaction into an argument. In that case not much will be accomplished.

If a customer is especially loud or abusive the service provider should never raise his or her voice. That only gives the customer an excuse to raise his or her voice further. Should a customer become especially abusive, let them rant, then apologize for the situation and calmly state that your goal is to get a thorough understanding of the situation in order to fix the problem in the best way possible. If one of your employees is encountering an abusive customer, have them refer the customer to you so you can resolve the issue.

Pro-Active and Effective Service Recovery

3. Empathize with the customer's situation

You've listened to the customer and understand their problem. If the problem is a mistake by your company, offer a genuine apology. Tell them you're sorry for the inconvenience and that you'll do what you can to see that it's fully rectified. It doesn't hurt to empathize with their plight (e.g. "You shouldn't have been treated that way. I would be angry too.") Let the customer know you can relate to their emotion and they'll immediately see you as an ally rather than someone who has to be convinced they were wronged.

4. Ask what would satisfy them

Ask them what the ideal outcome would be. Do they want the product replaced? Do they want some kind of remuneration? If you can provide their ideal solution you'll obviously contain the damage.

5. Offer the best solution or alternatives

Sometimes the customer's preferred solution is one that you can provide immediately. If so, correct the situation as fast as possible. If not, offer alternatives that you know are within your immediate control. If the customer is still unsatisfied then escalate their issue to someone with more authority.

Customer-focused leaders empower their employees with the authority to make recovery decisions on-the-spot. They know the faster the problem is resolved, the more satisfied the customer will become. This means ensuring that your staff clearly understand how far they can go to resolve a problem. It requires a leap of faith on the manager's part, but experience has shown, that experienced employees that fully understand what they can and cannot do, and how far they can go to impress a customer, rarely, if ever; "give away the farm".

6. Deliver more than the customer expects

Action

Look for some way to go beyond what the customer expects. For instance, in the example above the service manager provided the customer with a ride to the airport and delivered the car when she returned from business. If you not only correct the problem but also make a genuine effort to win the customer back, they will notice.

7. Follow up to confirm satisfaction

Action

Finally, don't just correct the problem. Follow up with the customer afterwards to see if they're satisfied. Offer additional services or products free of charge. Let them know that their satisfaction is truly your objective.

Pro-Active and Effective Service Recovery

Will this really win a customer back? In extreme circumstances, some customers can never be won back. However, most just want a fair, prompt resolution to their problem and they want to be treated with respect. Yes, you will win the majority of customers back for one simple reason. If you amaze the customer with an outstanding and fast response and provide a solution which exceeds their expectations, that's what they will remember.

The harsh reality is that no matter how hard you try, people are going to make mistakes.

Given the significant financial impact pro-active recovery can have on your business, it simply makes good sense to take whatever measures you can to ensure that when these mistakes occur, your employees recover quickly and in a manner which has a significant, positive impact on the customer.

Make it easy for your customers to complain. They are doing you a huge service by letting you know how you are doing.

Evaluate your Moments of Truth and identify pre-determined actions which your employees can take when predictable problems occur.

Assess the individual skill levels of your customer contact employees to ensure they have the knowledge and skills required to effectively deal with customers' complaints.

On the following two pages we have provided a worksheet that you can use to assess your staff.

You may also wish to evaluate your entire Customer Complaint Management process. How can this process be streamlined to ensure the fastest possible resolution of customer complaints? Depending on your business, you may wish to explore technology-based complaint management systems.

Ensure that you learn from those negative Critical Customer Incidents and take specific actions to align your processes to minimize or eliminate frequent and common types of complaints.

The financial benefits are staggering.

Pro-Active and Effective Service Recovery

Customer-Contact Employee Feedback Tool

Objective: Use this feedback tool to assess the service and recovery skills of your employees. As you observe your customer-contact employee interacting with a customer, evaluate him or her on the following criteria. Be sure to enter any comments on your observations that will assist the employee in further refining his/her skills.

Note: Review these tips for making the most efficient use of the evaluation tool.

1. Take some time to familiarize yourself with this tool and the questions before observing your employees. The more familiar you are with the questions it contains, the easier it will be to consistently and objectively evaluate your customer-contact staff.

2. Review the form with your employees and discuss the specifics of what you will be looking for and how and when the employee will be monitored.

3. Provide two levels of feedback. First, a high level, generic feedback session for all customer service associates - i.e. This is how we did overall..... Next, provide a second level feedback session for each individual customer-contact employee so he/she can see how they performed.

4. Determine a schedule for conducting customer service evaluations on a regular basis. Consider conducting this assessment quarterly. That allows time for the employee to react to feedback and improvement opportunities. A constant focus on customer assessments will reinforce your commitment to service and raise the quality of that service across the board.

5. Build in reinforcements. Consider transferring the role of customer assessments to your employees or a particular employee. Also, link the results of the customer assessment to employee compensation and rewards - i.e. those that score consistently high on service assessments should be rewarded for that accomplishment.

Pro-Active and Effective Service Recovery

Customer-Contact Employee Feedback Tool

1   **Greeting the customer**

	Employee made eye contact, was attentive and acknowledged the customer in a timely manner	Comments:
O Strongly Disagree		
O Disagree		
O Somewhat Disagree		
O Somewhat Agree		
O Agree		
O Strongly Agree		
O Could not evaluate		

	Employee showed an enthusiastic attitude towards the customer	Comments:
O Strongly Disagree		
O Disagree		
O Somewhat Disagree		
O Somewhat Agree		
O Agree		
O Strongly Agree		
O Could not evaluate		

	Employee greeted the customer warmly and offered an introduction	Comments:
O Strongly Disagree		
O Disagree		
O Somewhat Disagree		
O Somewhat Agree		
O Agree		
O Strongly Agree		
O Could not evaluate		

	Employee used the customer's name (if possible)	Comments:
O Strongly Disagree		
O Disagree		
O Somewhat Disagree		
O Somewhat Agree		
O Agree		
O Strongly Agree		
O Could not evaluate		

2   **Identifying customer needs or concerns**

	Employee allowed the customer time to speak	Comments:
O Strongly Disagree		
O Disagree		
O Somewhat Disagree		
O Somewhat Agree		
O Agree		
O Strongly Agree		
O Could not evaluate		

Pro-Active and Effective Service Recovery

O Strongly Disagree O Disagree O Somewhat Disagree O Somewhat Agree O Agree O Strongly Agree O Could not evaluate	Employee listened carefully to the customer describe their need/problem	Comments:
O Strongly Disagree O Disagree O Somewhat Disagree O Somewhat Agree O Agree O Strongly Agree O Could not evaluate	Employee assisted the customer in clarifying their need/problem by asking good open-ended questions	Comments
O Strongly Disagree O Disagree O Somewhat Disagree O Somewhat Agree O Agree O Strongly Agree O Could not evaluate	Employee assisted customer in identifying any constraints (i.e. price, ease of use, delivery/installation etc.)	Comments:

3	**Providing solutions to meet customer needs**	
O Strongly Disagree O Disagree O Somewhat Disagree O Somewhat Agree O Agree O Strongly Agree O Could not evaluate	Employee paraphrased the customer's need/problem	Comments:
O Strongly Disagree O Disagree O Somewhat Disagree O Somewhat Agree O Agree O Strongly Agree O Could not evaluate	Employee's assessment of the customer's need/problem was accurate	Comments:
O Strongly Disagree O Disagree O Somewhat Disagree O Somewhat Agree O Agree O Strongly Agree O Could not evaluate	Employee demonstrated product/service knowledge when offering the customer the benefits of the options/solutions	Comments:

Pro-Active and Effective Service Recovery

O Strongly Disagree O Disagree O Somewhat Disagree O Somewhat Agree O Agree O Strongly Agree O Could not evaluate	Employee presented product/service information in a manner the customer understood	Comments:
O Strongly Disagree O Disagree O Somewhat Disagree O Somewhat Agree O Agree O Strongly Agree O Could not evaluate	Employee offered the best possible product or service based on the customer's need/problem	Comments:

4	**Confirm customer's satisfaction with solutions offered**	
O Strongly Disagree O Disagree O Somewhat Disagree O Somewhat Agree O Agree O Strongly Agree O Could not evaluate	The customer was satisfied with the options/solutions presented	Comments:
O Strongly Disagree O Disagree O Somewhat Disagree O Somewhat Agree O Agree O Strongly Agree O Could not evaluate	Employee used positive phrases when dealing with the customer (e.g. Thank you, your welcome, please, I apologize, excuse me, Can I be of assistance, may I help you, It's been a pleasure helping you, Enjoy your selection, Do you have any suggestions for improving our service?)	Comments:
O Strongly Disagree O Disagree O Somewhat Disagree O Somewhat Agree O Agree O Strongly Agree O Could not evaluate	Employee avoided negative phrases (e.g. I can't help you, That's not our fault, You must be mistaken, You should have, You shouldn't have, What do you want me to do about it?, We don't handle that, There's nothing I can do, etc.)	Comments:
O Strongly Disagree O Disagree O Somewhat Disagree O Somewhat Agree O Agree O Strongly Agree O Could not evaluate	Employee used positive non-verbals when dealing with the customer (e.g. Make and maintain eye contact, smile, Allow a comfortable distance/space, Stop working on other things while speaking with the customer, Appear and sound enthusiastic, Maintain a neat, professional appearance, etc.)	Comments:

Pro-Active and Effective Service Recovery

O Strongly Disagree O Disagree O Somewhat Disagree O Somewhat Agree O Agree O Strongly Agree O Could not evaluate	Employee avoided negative non-verbals when dealing with the customer (e.g. Adverse facial expressions, rolling eyes, Talking over your shoulder or as you walk away, Working while you speak, Gesturing to the customer rather than speaking, Appearing bored, lethargic, etc.)	Comments:
	Additional items:	
O Strongly Disagree O Disagree O Somewhat Disagree O Somewhat Agree O Agree O Strongly Agree O Could not evaluate	Employee spoke in a clear, articulate manner which was easy for the customer to understand	Comments:
O Strongly Disagree O Disagree O Somewhat Disagree O Somewhat Agree O Agree O Strongly Agree O Could not evaluate	Employee completed the customer interaction in a timely manner	Comments:
O Strongly Disagree O Disagree O Somewhat Disagree O Somewhat Agree O Agree O Strongly Agree O Could not evaluate	Employee added extra value by delivering more than the customer expected	Comments

For more information regarding this and other assessment tools and service specific training, feel free to contact us. Our contact information is in the back of this book.

Reward and Recognition

Chapter 12

Characteristics of Successful, Customer-Focused Organizations:

"Provided recognition and reward for employees who exemplified stellar service."

A Human Resource manager was given the task of designing and implementing a Reward and Recognition program at the company she worked for. She decided to give the manager of each department two movie tickets and a certificate for dinner at a local restaurant. Each month the managers could give the award to one of their employees. The managers would consider each of their employees, and coworkers could nominate one another. During the first month, enthusiasm was high and lots of nominations were made.

- *"Tom helped me with a backlog of work when the computer was down."*
- *"Sandy processed 1,240 claims. A new record for the department."*
- *"Doug worked with some coworkers to improve the paper flow between engineering and drafting, but it was mostly his idea."*
- *"Mary showed a lot of team spirit by collecting donations for the March of Dimes."*

Managers selected winners from the nominations or selected someone they thought was worthy of a night on the town. For an added touch, the Human Resource manager had their names posted on the bulletin board in the lobby. It seemed a success, but then something happened. Employees starting complaining about the process:

- *"I don't know what I need to do to win that stupid thing - maybe I'll nominate myself."*
- *"I worked darn hard on that project last month and got nothing for it."*
- *"I didn't want my name posted in the lobby, how embarrassing."*
- *"Did you hear Doug won the award? His coworkers are mad because they worked just as hard on the same project."*
- *"Yeah - Sandy broke the record for claims processed, but I heard a ton of them came back with errors."*
- *"I worked every weekend to win that award and you mean Doris won it just for being a team player?"*

Over the next four months, nominations slowed to a trickle. Managers reported having difficulty finding employees they felt should win the award. They felt like they were rewarding mediocre performance. After a while the whole thing dried up and was quietly dismantled.

This story is extremely common. Well meaning managers institute a Reward and Recognition (R & R) program that actually <u>de-motivates</u> staff. The problem isn't a lack of intent or hard work. It's a lack of understanding regarding what makes these types of programs effective or ineffective.

This chapter:

- provides an outline for designing your own Reward and Recognition program
- includes a list of critical "Do's and Don'ts" for designing your Reward and Recognition Program

Reward and Recognition

Why is this important?

R&R programs are an important facet of providing employees with a satisfying, motivating work environment. Satisfied, motivated employees mean fewer problems for managers and more time to deal with other priorities. Many companies attempt R&R programs, but designed incorrectly they can actually have a detrimental effect on employees.

Critical Considerations

The first rule of Reward and Recognition is:

> <u>Recognize</u> **positive changes in employee behavior.**
> <u>Reward</u> **the consistent application of desired behaviors.**

Managers often confuse "reward" and "recognition". They <u>reward</u> people when they should be <u>recognizing</u> the efforts. Just because an employee does something once doesn't ensure he/she is going to consistently repeat that particular behavior. When you see someone trying a customer-focused behavior for the first time, make a big deal of it; acknowledge it, tell them what it was that they did which demonstrated the behavior you are encouraging and why this is valued. To use a familiar expression, "Catch them doing things right." Try to provide your recognition as close to the occurrence as possible.

Once you see that this type of behavior is consistently demonstrated by an employee and the results exemplify service excellence, that's the time to reward.

It's important to keep the intent of Reward and Recognition programs in focus. They should be just one way of saying "thank you," one way of reinforcing the behaviors and accomplishments you believe will ensure success. They can't replace personal, informal and on-going praise from a manager. In fact, research by Dr. Gerald Graham, Management Professor at Wichita State University, involving over a thousand employees in various companies found that managers who:

- personally thank employees for their efforts
- publicly acknowledge efforts
- reward outstanding performance with career growth
- document specific accomplishments of employees
- devote time in staff meetings to acknowledge high performers

... have the highest impact on motivation.

Reward and Recognition

A Model for Effective Reward Programs

Now let's take a look at a roadmap for designing your own Reward and Recognition program. There are a lot of potholes, so watch out! With some forethought you can design an effective program. Just be sure to follow these steps.

1. Determine what you are rewarding (Behaviors / Outcomes)

2. Determine your rewards

3. Determine how the program will be structured

4. Determine how you will pick the winner(s)

5. Determine how you will avoid "losers"

STEP 1: Determine what you are rewarding

It's not uncommon for managers to say that the objective of their Reward program is, "to recognize outstanding contributions and efforts" - or - "to reward efforts above and beyond normal job responsibilities." Sometimes managers don't want to limit nominations so they'll say "anything goes." If an employee feels a coworker did something great, that's cause enough to be nominated.

The problem with this broad approach is that employees don't really know <u>what they have to do</u> to receive the reward. Managers should use the reward program to reinforce performance and behaviors that support strategic objectives of the organization. This will be covered in more detail in step 4. While the focus of this book is creating a customer-focused organization, we did not want to limit our discussions to this alone. Here are some popular examples of strategic objectives:

Increasing productivity	The employee suggests several worthwhile improvements that removes unnecessary work, reduces mistakes, makes it easier for workers to do their job, etc.
Improving customer satisfaction and service	The employee is recognized by several customers for their outstanding help; the employee takes the initiative to satisfy an angry customer; the employee suggests several ways to improve customer service, etc.
Reducing operational expense	The employee identifies ways to reduce waste or ways to reduce overhead costs, supplier costs, etc.
Increasing revenue	The employee identifies ways to increase sales, expand product lines or increase margins, etc.

The key is to reward the specific behaviors and accomplishments by staff that achieves your strategic objectives. By doing so, you focus their attention on the keys areas that will make your organization successful.

Reward and Recognition

STEP 2: Determine your rewards

So what are you going to award to your top performers? A trip to Maui? A 20% raise? Their own company car? The best thing to do is ask your staff what they would value. There's nothing worse than rewarding people with things they don't want. This tends to have the opposite effect to what you are trying to accomplish. Once you have found out what will excite your staff, provide them with a range of options such as (but not limited to):

- ✓ *A day off*
- ✓ *Movie tickets and dinner*
- ✓ *Breakfast with executive management*
- ✓ *A Challenging project*
- ✓ *More responsibility or autonomy*
- ✓ *A Plaque or public recognition*
- ✓ *Money*

There are hundreds of specific examples. Some companies offer a continuum for rewards depending on the magnitude of the employee's contribution. This way even small efforts can be acknowledged. Remember...if you want to know what your employees would value as a reward... ask them.

STEP 3: Determine how the program will be structured

Your program needs some administrative guidelines, some operating rules that will keep it going and most importantly keep it consistent and equitable. Here are some considerations:

a) **Involve employees in designing the program.**
   - This will ensure that staff support the program and trust its integrity.

b) **Determine if employees will be nominated by peers, managers, or both**
   - Most companies encourage employees to participate in the nomination process.
   - Determine if the nominations are to be made by ballot or verbally, and what the process will be.

c) **Determine how the winner(s) will be selected**
   - Establish a selection committee.
   - Determine who should sit on the committee (managers, staff or both).
   - Determine if there will be multiple winners.
   - Empower the committee with the authority to ask managers and peers for more detail if necessary.
   - Determine how often recipients will be selected (monthly, quarterly, yearly).

Reward and Recognition

d) Determine how rewards will be offered

- Will smaller rewards go to other nominees (non-winners) for their efforts?

- Will it be a fixed reward or will there be options from which the winner(s) may choose?

e) Determine your budget

- What can your company or department afford to offer?

- If an employee's contributions result in cost savings, can that be translated to monetary rewards?

f) Determine if there will be public recognition or a ceremony of sorts

- Once the selection committee has chosen the recipient(s) how will they be notified?

- Will you hold a formal meeting/presentation?

- Will you communicate this in a company newsletter / bulletin board, etc.?

- Keep in mind that not everyone likes to be singled out in public. Others love the limelight. Try to avoid embarrassing someone unintentionally.

g) Determine how you will asses the effectiveness of your Reward program

- Some companies survey staff quarterly to get feedback on the work environment. Included in that survey are questions regarding the Reward program.

- It's also recommended that for the first 3 or4 months, someone other than the selection committee, review the documentation / justification from the selection committee by which recipients were selected to ensure consistency in the process.

h) Develop a schedule for the program

- When will the program begin?

- When will nominations be reviewed?

- When will the rewards be presented?

- When will the program be assessed?

- Who will administer the program?

STEP 4: Determine how you will pick the winner(s)

Perhaps the most difficult, yet most important step in designing your Reward program is establishing selection criteria. Without these, it's impossible to establish objectivity and credibility in the program. Employees will think it's luck, or worse, favoritism. In establishing criteria consider two areas: outcomes and behaviors.

Reward and Recognition

Outcomes are measurable indicators of productivity. For example:

- Reward the customer service representative(s) who handle the highest call volume and maintain a quality audit rating of at least 98% (Or improved the most).

- Reward the claims processor(s) who process the highest number of claims and maintain a quality audit rating of at least 99% (Or improved the most).

- Reward the salesperson(s) who generate the highest percentage increase in revenue for their prospective sales territories (Or improved the most).

- Reward Quality Improvement Teams who demonstrate measurable improvement in their work processes.

Behaviors are less tangible but just as important in accomplishing the strategic objectives of the company:..

- Reward "team players" - those who assist coworkers with problems, show support for coworkers and the unit, share information, assist in problem solving and maintain a friendly, approachable manner.

- Reward employees who are "risk takers" as demonstrated by suggesting new processes, attempting new initiatives, challenging management / peers, owning mistakes and volunteering for projects.

- Reward employees who demonstrate respect and integrity by owning up to errors, giving credit to others for efforts and ideas, and who take the time to say "thank you."

Clearly specify what it is that employees need to do or achieve. You can use any number of both outcome and behavioral objectives.

As for who selects the winner, that's also up to you. Some companies appoint an R&R committee made up of management. Others ask employees to run the show. In others it makes sense to have a single manager select the winner. There is no best answer. The important point it is, whoever selects the winner needs to make sure they are rewarding a legitimate, valuable, significant contribution.

Reward and Recognition

STEP 5: Determine how you will avoid "losers"

Unfortunately, by selecting a winner or winners there are, by default, losers. The last thing you want to do is motivate one winner and de-motivate everyone else; let's call them non-winners. There are several things you can do to avoid this pitfall:

a) **Establish clear, measurable, observable and tangible criteria.**

If you have clear criteria it'll be easier for non-winners to rationalize why they did not win the reward. This, along with communicating the justification for selecting the winner, is the best way to avoid a negative reaction from non-winners.

b) **Use a tiered approach in your program**

Offer smaller rewards to individuals and teams who have made some contribution.

c) **Tell non-winners what they could do differently**

Let your employees know where to improve. Further challenge them with a goal to better their performance.

d) **Don't select a winner....**

If the Review Committee feels that all nominees have made an admirable effort but that none truly standout, don't select a winner. Bold, yes but this can make a real statement. It raises the bar for performance and sends a clear message that the reward is no joke.

In addition to these Five Steps, here are a few more general considerations for running an effective reward and recognition program.

1. **Get the endorsement of your senior executive.**

The senior executive must convey the importance of the Reward program, and make clear the responsibility of both managers and staff to support it. It should sincerely be viewed as an honor to receive the reward.

2. **Never reward individuals or teams for mediocre contributions.**

If at some time you don't have any nominees who truly meet the criteria, don't reward anyone. Explain why. This will maintain the integrity of your program and keep the award meaningful.

3. **Have a mix of management and staff involved in designing the program, nominating and selecting the winner(s).**

This will encourage confidence in the program and maintain / facilitate a perception of objectivity.

Reward and Recognition

4. **Change the Reward program periodically.**

   Your criteria don't necessarily need to change unless your business practices have. But, periodically (yearly) change the theme. Reexamine your rewards and look for new, creative awards.

5. **Select a mid to upper level manager to oversee the program.**

   Companies will sometimes let an employee team oversee the program. These employees are capable of overseeing the program. The problem is that management support for the program begins to wane. Money for rewards gets tangled in administration, presentations /meetings get bumped from managers' schedules, and senior management doesn't communicate the importance of the Reward program.

6. **Remember: the mark of a Customer-Focused Leader is the ability to foster exceptional behavior in his or her employees.**

   A reward and recognition program is a relatively painless way to foster such behavior. Also, don't think that your department doesn't have the budget for such a program. Rewards need not be expensive to be effective. Sometimes a parking space with their name on it for a month, a luncheon, a Thank You letter they can share with their family or a hallway or conference room named after them is rewarding enough. It just needs to be fair and sincere.

Reward and Recognition

The Law of Unintended Effects

A sub-title to this section could be "Be Careful What You Wish For." When computers were first introduced into the workplace the big buzzword at the time was 'office automation'. One of the intended consequences of office automation was the reduction of use of paper. What happened instead was the increase in the use of paper. Now that people had the ability to generate their own documents everyone seemed to want their own hard copy.

You're all familiar with spam. That's an unintended effect of the proliferation of email.

When it comes to reward programs, an unintended effect is that it creates a situation which can cause a shift in focus for some people from the main reason you started the reward program (to reward the behavior you want to achieve your objectives) to winning the prize.

For example:

> *One company, which shall go nameless, wanted to reduce call wait times in their customer service call center. They established a reward program which focused on creating incentives for handling a higher volume of calls. Some people continued to handle about the same volume of calls while others increased their call volume by as much as 40%. The individuals who increased their call volumes received many accolades and rewards. Those that didn't increase call volumes were showing signs of frustration. This went on for some time. It seemed that the same people were getting rewarded every week. Then slowly but surely those in the bottom percentile began to improve their call volumes. At the same time, managers began to notice an incremental rise in the number of customer complaint calls, in particular, the volume of complaints about the call center. The numbers were not significant but they were increasing.*

> *On closer examination it was determined that those employees who had initially increased their call volumes were spending only a fraction of the time on the telephone with each customer. These customers were not getting the help they needed and rather than being satisfied they were being irritated. Since most of these customers didn't think complaining would do any good, it took quite some time before the problem came to light. Those employees who did not initially increase their call volumes had up to that point been getting high marks when it came to the high levels customer satisfaction. Their calls took longer but the results were significantly better. Over time, these employees began to spend less time with customers so they too could be eligible for the rewards.*

> *Customer wait times improved significantly. The quality of the calls and the company's service reputation however, dropped like a lead balloon. Clearly this is not the outcome or effect the managers wanted. It was an unintended effect of focusing their rewards on the wrong things.*

People are wonderfully complex creatures. That's good and bad. There will always be some people who will go after rewards at the expense of others, particularly if the rewards are compelling enough. That's not to say that reward programs are not a valuable tool. But if you are going to use rewards, ensure that you carefully consider what you are rewarding. Always ensure that:

- there is a quality measure tied to the behavior you are rewarding
- your rewards criteria is tied back to your service values
- your measures are fair, accurate and objective
- your customers' feedback is included in your evaluation criteria

Reward and Recognition

In summary here are things to keep in mind when planning and administering your Reward Program:

Recognize positive changes in employee behavior – catch people doing things right and recognize the effort in order to reinforce and encourage repetition of the behavior.

Reward the consistent application of desired behaviors.

Motivation is a personal thing - personalize rewards or offer options to choose from.

Be timely and specific - recognition and rewards are most effective when they can be easily linked to an accomplishment as close to the actual occurrence as possible.

Avoid "losers" - be sure to recognize (appreciate) all efforts, even if the accomplishments vary in significance.

Reward the important things - identify specific behaviors and accomplishments that support your strategic direction.

Change your program as necessary - to rekindle interest, the theme or delivery of your program may have to change. Don't just yank the plug on one and start another. Communicate the transition and emphasize the continued importance of reward and recognition.

Remember the Law of Unintended Effects

Measuring Operational and Service Quality

Chapter 13

Characteristics of Successful, Customer-Focused Organizations:

"Used data to measure the efficiency of internal processes."

As we discussed earlier, customers have some pretty typical expectations (satisfactors) common to most businesses:

Service Cosmetics	Are service associates friendly and empathic to customer needs?
Service Accuracy	Can customers get an accurate answer to their questions and a resolution to their problems?
Service Accessibility	Is it easy for customers to get service and assistance?
Product / Service Reliability	Does the product or service the customer purchased work as intended?
Cost Competitive	Is the customer satisfied they paid a reasonable price for the product or service?

You may have others, but chances are these categories cover most or all of your products and services. If you're advanced enough to measure these satisfactors you're probably ahead of many other companies. But let's turn it up a notch. What happens when:

- you're losing customers because your service associates are unfriendly or impatient?
- complaints keep escalating because customers can't get a clear answer to their problems?
- you're losing orders and customers because it takes too long to get through to a service representative?
- service calls increase because customers are having problems with your product?
- sales drop because your products are priced too high so you lower prices, then can't make a profit?

You need some measurements to tell you how things are operating internally and where problems exist.

This chapter:

- provides a case study that illustrates the connection between service and operational measures
- offers examples of operational measures
- explains how these operational measures can be used as the foundation of your improvement efforts
- provides an exercise to help you identify your operational and service measures
- provides an exercise for identifying your service and quality improvement readiness

Measuring Operational and Service Quality

Why is this important?

Highly successful Customer-Focused Organizations use data to measure the efficiency of internal processes and make changes which positively impact the customer experience. A manager that has a good set of operational measures by which to monitor business efficiency is in an enviable position. Now he or she can pinpoint problems and make real improvements to the business or department. Contrast that with the manager who has no idea where problems are occurring so fixes everything by hiring more staff or spending more money. Soon, that manager is out of business.

Identifying Operational Measures

Every company needs to have a way to measure the efficiency of its work processes. Without data, activities and priorities fall out of focus. Let's look at a case study based on real events that describes how a company can use operational measures to not only improve, but in this case stay alive!

Case Study: Cybersaver

Background:

When it first started Cybersaver, a high volume technical retailer, was touted as a no frills, cost competitive, service oriented supplier of computers and computer accessories. With the explosion of the Internet and the proliferation of computer technology, consumers were desperate for an outfit like Cybersaver. They made it easy to shop by phone or the Internet. Cybersaver carried a limited number of brands so consumers weren't overwhelmed with options. Brands were selected based on reports from independent consumer and product research firms. Stores didn't carry much inventory. Instead orders were shipped from a network of supply houses or directly from manufacturers.

Their sales process was seemingly simple. Orders taken at a store, by phone or via the Internet were funneled to a central dispatching system. Purchases were shipped within 24-48 hours. At first Cybersaver did a booming business. Customers liked the personal support they received from knowledgeable service reps. The process for purchasing products was simple and most orders were cut, filled, shipped and received within five business days.

Things began to unravel

As the volume of orders increased, the time to fill those orders was taking longer and longer. Now instead of five business days to deliver an order, it was taking up to two weeks. More customers were calling about the status of their merchandise and telephone wait times increased. To make matters worse there was an increase in technical problems when Cybersaver introduced a new product line. Management cracked the whip to get orders filled faster but that only led to mistakes, increasing returns and phone calls. The customer service manager started to watch lunch breaks and reprimanded those who were tardy. Staff meetings and in-service training were cancelled to keep customer service reps at their stations. That only backfired when some got fed up and resigned.

Somehow a work environment that was previously productive and team oriented degenerated into detached individuals unconcerned about what went on outside their cubicles. The frustration of the service reps was reflected in the tone of their voice and their dwindling empathy for customer issues. In a knee jerk reaction the service manager set a standard that the average talk time per phone call should not exceed three minutes. By doing so he thought more calls could be handled and the wait times would decrease. He was wrong. By cutting calls short, service reps made more mistakes and the deluge of calls continued. Since many problems couldn't be resolved in the three minutes, many reps

Measuring Operational and Service Quality

offered to call the customer back - something that usually didn't happen. Customers resented being rushed off the phone when they needed answers to their problems. Sales plummeted.

The irony is, once sales dropped, service reps were able to handle the volume. However, management was on the hot seat to boost sales.

What happened?

This is a great example of how inefficiencies in your work environment ultimately impact your customer. It's like the old saying, "One papercut ain't gonna kill you, but 10,000 will". The "process" at Cybersaver worked to a degree. When it exceeded a certain capacity, however, it overheated and broke down.

If managers at Cybersaver had a set of operational measures, they could have either nipped problems in their early stages or addressed them at their root cause.

Cybersaver solicited the help of a management consulting firm specializing in process improvement and business efficiency. First the consultants examined data gathered weekly by the Cybersaver service manager. He monitored the following:

- Volume of calls
- Average response time (average time for someone to answer a call)
- Number of calls abandoned (times callers hung up after waiting more than 20 seconds for a service rep)
- Volume of calls per service representative
- Average talk time per call and per service rep

These were a good start but they weren't very helpful in pinpointing operational problems. For instance:

Volume of calls	Why were calls increasing? Orders were up but certainly not all the calls were for orders. Many were callers who had problems and questions.
Average response time	The average response time had increased dramatically from 12 seconds to 125 seconds (over 2 minutes) in just four months. But why?
Number / percent of calls abandoned	The number of calls abandoned had increased apparently because the response time had increased. Again, why had the wait time increased?
Volume of calls per service representative	The number of calls handled per representative had increased but only because management was pressuring them to improve response time and lower the abandonment rate. While a good indication that service reps were busy, this data didn't help uncover any operational problems.

Measuring Operational and Service Quality

Average talk time per call and per service rep

This is perhaps the one piece of data that could indicate an improvement opportunity. Like most telephone service units Cyberspace used an ACD system (Automatic Call Distribution). Incoming calls went into a bank and the next available rep took the call. Since one could assume calls came in randomly, and that the types of calls were random (orders, complaints, questions, etc.) it was probable reps were handling similar calls. If some reps had significantly higher talk times they probably needed additional training on how to handle calls and problems.

Instead the consultants suggested focusing on more operational measures. For instance:

Problem	Operational Measure
Call volume had increased but what types of calls were reps getting? To check the status of an order? To order more products? To report a product problem? A payment problem? Receipt of an incorrect order? This data would help pinpoint problems.	Volume of calls by type
Where were backlogs occurring? For instance were orders taken but waiting to be filled? Were orders filled but waiting to be shipped? Again, this would suggest an improvement opportunity in the workflow.	Volume of backlogs
How many calls were due to the fact that something wasn't done correctly the first time?	Incidence of rework
Were service reps handling inquiries in the most efficient manner? Did all service reps have adequate product knowledge? Why were some able to maintain a shorter average talk time? Were all service reps courteous and customer oriented?	Grade service reps on call efficiency
Was the computer system responsive? Were delays caused because service reps were dealing with a slow computer system?	Measures of system response time
Were service reps burned out or de-motivated? The situation certainly suggested that was the fact. This is especially crucial to customer service because the quality of customer service is proportional to the quality of employee relations.	Measures of employee satisfaction

Measuring Operational and Service Quality

These operational measures now gave the manager red flags suggesting opportunities for improvement. For instance:

Volume of calls by type	Data showed many calls were related to a new line of high speed modems, color monitors and office software. This focused efforts on improving or eliminating those products. A high volume of billing questions hinted at problems with the invoicing system.
Volume of backlogs	Data showed that orders were filled within a reasonable time after they were placed. However, backlogs were growing at the distribution centers suggesting the root cause of the delay was there.
Incidence of rework	There were a fairly significant number of calls pertaining to orders that were incomplete or inaccurate. This suggested that the warehouse was turning around the orders quickly, but unfortunately, they were making mistakes.
Grade service reps on call monitoring	The Cybersaver manager randomly selected two calls per service rep/per week and monitored them. Each rep was assessed using a standard tool to identify improvement opportunities.
System response time	Over the period of four weeks several service reps were asked to time the response time of the system (time between screens) at standard intervals (9:00am, 11:00am, 1:00pm, and 3:00pm). Data showed a significant impact at 9:00am and 11:00am when call volume was highest. This led to additional hardware and a staggered break/lunch schedule which provided better support.
Measures of employee satisfaction	The consultants conducted a survey to assess employee morale and sure enough there were problems. Many resented the management atmosphere. They felt that management did not seek their input or suggestions, changes were badly implemented, and communicated and there was little reward for doing a good job. This led to individual consulting with the manager to improve his management style and to build opportunities for employee involvement into the environment.

The result...

Over the course of four months the customer service function improved dramatically. Four months may seem like along time, but this is the reality. Usually there isn't one big fix that's going to cause productivity and service quality to skyrocket. The problems tend to be smaller but accumulate over time until the process becomes buried in inefficiencies. Again, you can die from 10,000 papercuts.

Measuring Operational and Service Quality

Examples of Operational Measures

Since all businesses are made up of work processes and since the efficiency of those work processes share common characteristics it's possible to identify universal operational measures. The context of your measure may differ – e.g.: retail vs. medical vs. engineering, etc. But see if you can identify with the commonalties in these fairly universal examples of operational measures:

Response time	This is more of a performance measure or symptom of how effectively a function operates but it doesn't pinpoint problems. If you manage a hotel and customers are complaining that room service is taking too long you've got a symptom but have to dig deeper.
Service Cosmetics	Whether or not your service staff is friendly and empathic to customer needs can be considered an operational measure. Things like a friendly greeting, effective listening, a respectful tone and a supportive closing are all part of the cosmetic presentation of service. These are all things that can be monitored. If you fail at the cosmetic presentation of service it will have a direct impact on your customers.
Volume/Types of problems	It's a common complaint by managers, "I spend all day fixing problems and can't get any real work done!" If you step back a moment and quantify the type of problems you're handling you can begin to zero in on the root cause(s).
Rework	Rework suggests something wasn't done right the first time. Some business scholars have estimated that the amount of work in a typical company considered rework is about 35%! In any case, every business suffers from it and it's one of the biggest indicators of improvement opportunities.
Backlogs	Backlogs are any points in a process where work backs up. Standing in line at the airport. Waiting for your mortgage approval. Waiting for products to be shipped. Backlogs make it easy to find problems. Whatever step in your process is after the backlog – it's probably a bottleneck.
Individual differences	Some employees are great at sales while their peers are mediocre. Some can handle a tremendous amount of phone calls while others can barely keep up. Some can process paperwork quickly and accurately while others create more problems than they're worth. Assess your employees. Rank them based on job requirements. Just as the call monitoring tool can help you assess customer service reps, you should have some way of identifying individual differences among your employees. First, it makes performance management easier; but, it can also be used to pinpoint training needs among your less productive staff. Identify the qualities that make some employees stand out then *ask them* to help train others!
Employee Morale	According to some consultants 80% of the opportunity for improvement in business lies not in automation or computers but in people. The importance of employee morale and motivation cannot be stressed enough. If you have a staff that's willing to put in 110% effort, that likes to come to work, that is challenged, motivated and proud of their accomplishments there is nothing your business cannot accomplish. Nothing.

Measuring Operational and Service Quality

Here's an exercise to help you examine the measures you currently have in place as well as identify additional measures that you want to put into place.

Operational and Service Quality Measures

On a fresh sheet of paper, jot down your responses to each of the questions provided. Depending on your responses be sure to give yourself lots of room for your responses.

Consider the following questions:

1. What operational measures do you currently have in place?

2. What data do these measures provide?

3. Can this data be used to make customer-focused improvements?

4. Are there any gaps in the data you are currently gathering?

5. What additional data requirements need to be added to these existing measures?

6. Based on your responses thus far, what changes do you need to make to your existing measures?

7. What do you need to do to ensure everyone understands these changes?

8. Based on what was covered in this chapter, what additional measures do you need to put in place?

9. How will you put these measures into practice?

10. Are there any foreseeable unintended effects as a result of using the amended or new measures?

Some say, you get what you measure. A word to the wise... you get what you pay attention to.

Measuring Operational and Service Quality

The reason we measure is so that we can learn and use the information we gather to make significant long-term improvements to our business. Why not take a few minutes now to assess your operational and service Improvement Readiness? This assessment is divided into six steps.

Step 1 - How do you measure quality?

Step 2 - How are you doing?

Step 3 - Where / how can we do better?

Step 4 - Implement the Improvement

Step 5 - Verify the Improvement

Step 6 - Maintain the Improvement

After you have completed this assessment you will find a page which will help you to score your results.

Exercise

13.2

Improvement Readiness Assessment

Review each question on the following 6 pages and select one rating which corresponds to each question. You will notice some points to consider which are there to help you when considering your rating. At the end of the assessment, follow the instructions provided.

Step 1 - How do you measure quality?

1. How well do you understand the service and product expectations of your customer(s) - Long and short term?	
O No understanding = 1 pt O Little = 2 pts O Average = 3 pts O Good = 4 pts O Excellent understanding = 5 pts	Points to consider Could you list the top 5 concerns customers have about your products or services? Do you have a process for gathering customer feedback on your products and/or services? Have your products and/or services evolved as your customers' needs have changed?
2. Are you assuming you know the expectations of your customers or have you verified their needs?	
O Assuming we know = 1 pt O Half and half = 3 pts O Definitely verified = 5 pts	Points to consider When you lose a customer do you have a process for finding out why they left or chose your competitor? Have your indicators of customer satisfaction shown steady improvement? Have you identified the unique needs of different customer segments or do you focus on one set of customer measurements?

Measuring Operational and Service Quality

3. Do you have a process to measure whether or not you're meeting customers' expectations for service and product quality?

O No process = 1 pt O Not very effective = 2 pts O Effective = 3 pts O Very effective = 4 pts O Extremely effective = 5 pts	Points to consider Do you have a report card that measures how satisfied your customers are with your products and services? Is there a strong correlation between your measures of service and productivity and your customer retention and growth?

4. Do staff know how they impact the customers' perception of quality?

O Little or no understanding = 1 pt O Some understanding = 3 pts O Full understanding = 5 pts	Points to consider Do the performance goals and objectives for each of your employees include references to their customers? Do your employees have a chance to interact directly with customers - either external or internal? Do you reward your employees for providing outstanding customer service - to either external or internal customers?

5. How well do your departments understand the quality expectations of departments they interface with? (internal partners)

O Little or no understanding = 1 pt O Some understanding = 3 pts O Full understanding = 5 pts	Points to consider Among other deliverables, are your department managers evaluated on how well they support other departments? Could your staff tell you the priorities and quality measures of the departments with which they interface? When changes are made in one department do you usually notice problems or disruptions in other departments?

6. Do you measure the quality of work processes internally (volume of work, accuracy, mistakes, rework etc.)?

O No measurements = 1 pt O Some measurements = 3 pts O Excellent measurements = 5 pts	Points to consider Have you identified measurements for quality between your departments - i.e., how well do your departments support one another? Do you track rework/mistakes and the timeliness of work as it flows between your departments? Do you have management mechanisms in place (i.e., teams, quality resources, etc.) that monitor the efficiency of work processes that cut across departments?

Points Sub-total:	

Measuring Operational and Service Quality

Step 2 - How are you doing?

7. How would you rate the effectiveness of reports available for managing your operations? - i.e. do you have a report card that tells you how well your company is performing?

- O No reports = 1 pt
- O Not very effective = 2 pts
- O Somewhat effective = 3 pts
- O Effective = 4 pts
- O Very effective reporting = 5 pts

Points to consider

Are you confident in the reliability of your reports?

Are you comfortable making decisions based on your operational reports?

Does your staff, management or peers challenge the validity of your operational reports?

8. Do you have quality reports which will show (rework, errors, backlogs, turnaround times, accuracy checks improvements in your operations?

- O Little or no reporting = 1 pt
- O Some reporting = 3 pts
- O Excellent reporting = 5 pts

Points to consider

Can you say with confidence whether or not you've made measurable improvements in your operations?

Do you have data that can tell you the exact points where your work processes need improvement?

9. How effective is your process for gathering regular feedback from customers?

- O No process = 1 pt
- O Not very effective = 2 pts
- O Effective = 3 pts
- O Very effective = 4 pts
- O Extremely effective = 5 pts

Points to consider

Do you have a way to validate the reliability of your customer feedback? Are you comfortable making decisions based on your customer feedback?

Do you have a standard set of reports that track/trend customer feedback or do you get the information ad hoc?

10. How effectively do you use feedback from customers to improve your business?

- O No process = 1 pt
- O Not very effective = 2 pts
- O Effective = 3 pts
- O Very effective = 4 pts
- O Extremely effective = 5 pts

Points to consider

Do you have a way to analyze customer feedback to uncover opportunities for improvement? Do you have a regular process to analyze the data? Do you have people dedicated to that responsibility?

11. Do you know how well you are doing relative to your competitors?

- O Little or no understanding = 1 pt
- O Some understanding = 3 pts
- O Full understanding = 5 pts

Points to consider

Have you identified your key competitors? Do you know the significant differences between your products and services and theirs?

What data do you have on your competitors? What process do you have to regularly gather that data and review it?

12. Do you know the top 3 complaints your customers have of your product or service?

- O No idea = 1 pt
- O Some idea = 3 pts
- O Full understanding = 5 pts

Points to consider

Can you name the significant complaints customers have about your business, products or services? If so, how do you know?

Can you describe the problems specifically enough to take action or are they more like symptoms of a problem?

Points Sub-total:

Measuring Operational and Service Quality

Step 3 - Where / how can we do better?

13. How well do you understand the workflows between departments (from the workers' perspective)? - i.e. Do you have clearly defined steps/processes for completing work?	
O No understanding = 1 pt O Little = 2 pts O Average = 3 pts O Good = 4 pts O Excellent understanding = 5 pts	Points to consider Do you have an actual workflow diagram that details processes and procedures between departments? Do your departments have clearly defined goals and expectations of one another?

14. How well do you understand the root cause of problems in your operations? - i.e. Do you fix problems and eliminate them or do you just work harder or longer hours?	
O No understanding = 1 pt O Little = 2 pts O Average = 3 pts O Good = 4 pts O Excellent understanding = 5 pts	Points to consider How often do you fix the same problems over and over? How often do you approve overtime or "throw bodies" at a problem to fix it - temporarily?

15. How often are problems dealt with by calling for overtime or extra personnel?	
O Very often = 1 pt O Sometimes = 3 pts O Rarely = 5 pts	Points to consider Do you hear employees complaining about long work hours? Do you see a lot of people taking work home with them? Do you find your department/business spending so much time on problems that it's interfering with your ability to service customers and/or sell products?

16. How often do you prioritize (using data) problem areas so the most relevant problems are addressed?	
O Rarely = 1 pt O Sometimes = 3 pts O Frequently = 5 pts	Points to consider Can you or your managers name the top service or production issues in your department or business? Are you able to demonstrate with data the magnitude of your problems? Are you able to demonstrate measurable improvements in your department or business?

17. How often do you use a structured approach to problem solving?	
O Rarely = 1 pt O Sometimes = 3 pts O Frequently = 5 pts	Points to consider In your typical meetings do you just "discuss" problems and eventually arrive at solutions, or do you use structured techniques (process mapping, decision matrices, brainstorming, cause & effect diagramming, cost benefit analysis, etc.) to prioritize problems and identify alternatives? When you fix a problem does it typically stay fixed or do the same problems typically flare up again and again?

18. How often do you find yourself dealing with the same backlog of work or mistakes?	
O Frequently = 1 pt O Sometimes = 3 pts O Rarely = 5 pts	Points to consider Do you often feel like you're managing problems day-to-day - i.e., throwing people and dollars at the same problems - or do you feel you're constantly improving efficiency? Have you assigned people the permanent responsibility of dealing with backlogs and mistakes on a regular basis?
Points Sub-total:	

Measuring Operational and Service Quality

Step 4 - Implement the Improvement

19. How well do you understand and address the dynamics of managing change (i.e. staff have to first understand the problem and why change is necessary, staff have to be involved in fixing problems, managers have to be involved closely in coaching / training staff so mistakes are used constructively and not ingrained etc.)?

O No understanding = 1 pt O Little = 2 pts O Average = 3 pts O Good = 4 pts O Excellent understanding = 5 pts	Points to consider Do you take time to explain the rationale for changes to your staff or do you typically just make changes and expect them to "roll with it?" How often do you ask for staff input on changes? Do you provide extra support (training, supervision, discussion, patience) to staff after you've implemented a change to their work load or process?

20. How effective is your change management process (i.e. changes prioritized & communicated, risk and impact determined, multiple changes coordinated effectively, etc.)?

O Not effective = 1 pt O Somewhat = 2 pts O Average = 3 pts O Good = 4 pts O Very Effective = 5 pts	Points to consider When you're planning a change for your department or business do you have a clear, consistent process for weighing the risks and impacts of the change? How often do you find yourself or your staff reacting to problems you hadn't expected after changes occur? Do staff complain of "too many changes" or "constant change"?

21. How effective are you at implementing a new workflow/process without negatively impacting other parts of your business?

O Not effective = 1 pt O Somewhat = 2 pts O Average = 3 pts O Good = 4 pts O Very Effective = 5 pts	Points to consider When you implement a change do you think about the departments and processes you interface with so you can determine the exact impact on them? Do other departments or managers complain about changes in your department that impact them? How many of your operational or service problems occur at interfaces between your department and others?

22. How effective are you at developing an implementation plan for changing workflows / processes, (i.e. address transition of work in progress, determining impact of changes, training staff, etc.)?

O Not effective = 1 pt O Somewhat = 2 pts O Average = 3 pts O Good = 4 pts O Very Effective = 5 pts	Points to consider Do you have a documented plan when you make significant changes? When making a significant change do you make accommodations so that work in progress can be folded easily into the new process? Do you prepare staff before the change occurs?

23. How often do you confirm that changes to policies and procedures are exercised correctly by all staff?

O Rarely = 1 pt O Sometimes = 3 pts O Frequently = 5 pts	Points to consider Do you check with staff after a change to make sure the change is being exercised consistently and correctly? Do you update policies, procedures, job descriptions, training materials, measurements, etc., after a change?

Points Sub-total:	

Measuring Operational and Service Quality

Step 5 - Verify the Improvement

24. How often do you validate (using data) that a change really led to improvement?	
O Rarely = 1 pt O Sometimes = 3 pts O Frequently = 5 pts	Points to consider When you fix a problem or make an improvement do you measure the outcome so that you can say with confidence - "We fixed that."? Do you have measurement systems that track productivity and efficiency of your key processes?
25. How often do you continue to monitor a change in the workflow (Quality Assurance) to ensure the process flows smoothly as opposed to dealing with flare ups?	
O Rarely = 1 pt O Sometimes = 3 pts O Frequently = 5 pts	Points to consider Do you have regular measures of efficiency (i.e., how well are your work processes working) that you watch for signs of problems or do you typically react to problems?
26. How many of the areas in your operations report improvements on a regular basis?	
O Not many = 1 pt O Some = 3 pts O Most = 5 pts	Points to consider Do you or your managers report regularly (e.g., weekly, monthly, or quarterly) on the same measures of efficiency? Can you demonstrate unequivocally that your department or business is constantly improving even if only in small increments?
Points Sub-total:	

Measuring Operational and Service Quality

Step 6 - Maintain the Improvement

27. How often are written policies / procedures as well as training and orientation material updated when changes occur?

O Rarely = 1 pt O Sometimes = 3 pts O Frequently = 5 pts	Points to consider Do you have documented policies and procedures as well as training materials? If you pulled out your policies/procedures, training material, etc., right now - how accurate would they be?

28. How often are performance appraisals and job descriptions updated as work processes change?

O Rarely = 1 pt O Sometimes = 3 pts O Frequently = 5 pts	Points to consider Do you have documented job descriptions? Do you conduct performance appraisals? If yes, to either of the above, how accurate are the documents right now?

29. How effectively do you communicate successful Quality Improvement efforts to all staff?

O Not effective = 1 pt O Somewhat = 2 pts O Average = 3 pts O Good = 4 pts O Very Effective = 5 pts	Points to consider Do you regularly tell staff about improvements in your department or business? Do you challenge staff to find more ways to improve service or productivity even after you've fixed a particular problem?

30. How effectively do you reward (equitably) employee efforts and contributions to Quality Improvement?

O Not effective = 1 pt O Somewhat = 2 pts O Average = 3 pts O Good = 4 pts O Very Effective = 5 pts	Points to consider Do you specifically recognize contributions employees make to identifying and fixing problems via their performance evaluation, bonuses or recognition programs, etc? If so, how consistently? Do employees approach you with ideas for improvement or do they only involve themselves when you bring a problem to their attention?

31. How effective is your process for re-evaluating and raising your quality standards after an improvement is made?

O Not effective = 1 pt O Somewhat = 2 pts O Average = 3 pts O Good = 4 pts O Very Effective = 5 pts	Points to consider Do you set new improvement targets that continuously challenge your department or business (not just goals - but improvement goals) to reach new levels of efficiency and service?

Points Sub-total:

Measuring Operational and Service Quality

Scoring

Add up the points for your responses for each category and place the sub-total in the areas provided in each category. Record these sub-totals in the spaces provided below.

Step 1 - How do you measure quality? (Questions 1-6) [possible 30 pts]

Sub-total:_____

Step 2 - How are you doing? (Questions 7-12) [possible 30 pts]

Sub-total:_____

Step 3 - Where / how can we do better? (Questions 13-18) [possible 30 pts]

Sub-total:_____

Step 4 - Implement the Improvement (Questions 19-23) [possible 25 pts]

Sub-total:_____

Step 5 - Verify the Improvement (Questions 24-26) [possible 15 pts]

Sub-total:_____

Step 6 - Maintain the Improvement (Questions 27-31) [possible 25 pts]

Sub-total:_____

Your Total Score

Best Possible Score = 155 points

Interpreting Your Score

Below 60 — Your score suggests that you need to make major improvements in your Service and Quality Improvement processes – if you don't have a formal process in place, it's time to create one.

60 to 89 — Your score suggests that there is some evidence of Service and Quality Improvement processes; however major improvements are needed in all areas.

90-119 — Your score suggests that you have average Service and Quality Improvement processes in place - focus on areas rated lowest in the assessment.

120 to 155 — Your score suggests that you have excellent Service and Quality Improvement processes - focus on demonstrating continuous improvement.

Measuring Operational and Service Quality

In summary, you are probably thinking that this is simply too much for you to do yourself. After all, you are already overworked and underappreciated. This kind of activity is perfect for building team service awareness and getting your team involved in their role as service providers.

Keep in mind, there is a better than average chance that many on your team already know what is important to your customers, what processes work, what ones cause problems, what measures are realistic and what will impress customers. So use all this brain power to get the job done.

Don't be surprised if as you go through this exercise, you identify operational processes which are not customer-friendly and which actually prevent the delivery of exceptional service. When you do encounter **these**:

- analyze the process
- determine why it doesn't contribute to enhancing the customer experience
- determine what needs to be done to change it, and then
- change the process to make it more customer friendly

Above all:

- ensure that everyone understands what you are measuring
- why you are measuring it
- what they need to do differently in order to be successful, and
- what to do when they encounter flaws in your processes which contribute to poor service

In the context of developing a Customer-Focused Organization, it is critical to have measurements in place that give you up-to-date data which you can use to improve your processes and practices in a way which, from your customers' perspective, add value and make it easier to do business with you.

Conclusion

Chapter 14

You probably realized, by the time you got to around page 32 of this book that creating a customer-focused organization will not make you feel any less overworked. In fact it will take more work, long-term commitment and a passion for excellence. We have covered a great deal of territory in this book and in some ways we have only scratched the surface. If, however, you invest your time in implementing what we have covered here, you will see results. There is no doubt that creating a customer-focused organization will have a direct and positive impact on your bottom line. This is an investment in your future success.

For those of you who view training as a cost, you may want to rethink this notion. Your staff need to learn what they can do differently in order to succeed with your customers. Investing in developing your staff to deliver service excellence is critical. The leadership you provide will make or break your ability to create a truly customer-focused organization.

You have two choices:

- Do nothing knowing that your existing and more profitable customers have taken their business elsewhere before you find out about it and leave you powerless to do anything about it, or

- Decide to make a difference by creating a customer-focused company and watch your company, department or organization flourish.

Should you decide to make a difference, use the exercises and tools provided in this book to create and execute your own plan of action.

On the following three pages we have included and Action Items Checklist to help you develop your Customer-Focused Improvement Strategy and Plan. If you would like a more detailed step-by-step process we have one last suggestion.

Get our *Customer Focus Companion.* Included in this e-Book you will find a highly structured personal action planning tool to help you identify what you would like to do in order to put what you have learned as a result of completing this book into tangible action. We have also included an overview of an effective service team structure, several group problem solving tools and a series of 14 highly structured meeting guides to assist you in training and coaching your employees in the concepts required to create your Customer-Focused Organization.

Now as far as feeling underappreciated; when you have successfully created a customer-focused organization your employees will appreciate it. Your boss, shareholders or company owners will appreciate it. Your suppliers and vendors will appreciate it. And most importantly,

...your customers will appreciate it.

Conclusion

Here is a checklist of major action items to help you develop and implement your Customer-Focused strategy. **This is not a linear process**. Many of the steps below can and should be done on parallel tracks.

Critical Actions Checklist		**Date to be completed by**

1	Develop a business case
	  ✓ Determine the financial gains associated with increasing customer loyalty
	  ✓ Determine the financial consequences associated with poor service	

2	Determine your service vision and values
	  ✓ Connect to existing corporate vision and mission, or
	  ✓ If there is no vision or mission, create your service vision and values	

3	Determine if you will form a committee to work with you on development, roll-out and on-going support of strategy
	  ✓ Who should be on committee
	  ✓ Time commitment
	  ✓ Decision making authority
	  ✓ Roles and responsibilities
	  ✓ Invite team members to work with you on implementation
	  ✓ Determine and communicate goals, roles and responsibilities of implementation team members	

4	Determine preliminary budget forecast	

5	Develop your process for creating a "shared vision"
	  ✓ Company wide, small groups, or representative sampling
	  ✓ What can you do to encourage maximum participation in a time efficient manner?
	  ✓ Or will you include this step as part of the training?	

6	Develop a communication plan for how you will communicate all aspects of your CF strategy on an ongoing basis
	  ✓ How will you introduce staff to your plan?
	  ✓ How will you ensure that staff are constantly aware of what is happening and how they are doing?	

7	Assess the current level of internal cooperation and partnership ✓ This would be a good time to use the Service Climate Survey process	
8	Assess service mind-set and skills training needs ✓ Identify service performance gaps and specific training needs (all staff)	
9	Assess current level of customer-focused leadership including yourself and your managers and supervisors	

Conclusion

10	Reevaluate budget to ensure sufficient resources are set aside based on all needs identified.	
11	Develop your training plan for management and non-management ✓ Ensure that the Customer Focused Leadership gaps are identified and establish training to fill these gaps as your first priority ✓ Ensure that at the very least the items described in the chapter on training are covered for all staff	
12	Implement your "Shared Vision" process ✓ Do groups or as part of initial training	
13	Develop strategy and implement on-going plan for Listening to the Voice of the Customer ✓ Identify what methods you will use to know your customers ✓ Identify what methods you will use to know your competition ✓ Establish a process for how you will take what is learned and implement changes ✓ Begin listening	
14	Identify company wide minimum service standards	
15	Review existing performance management system and modify to reflect service values and standards	
16	Review hiring process and ensure hiring practices include customer focus requirements	
17	Determine Reward and Recognition program and processes	
18	Determine overall measurement process and plan to evaluate service performance improvement	
19	Roll out initial training either formal classroom training or via weekly or bi-weekly meetings ✓ Formal training is best for larger groups or organization wide. ✓ If only for a small department or company you may wish to do this in the form of 1 hour meetings every couple of weeks Once training is done each work group, team or department should then meet at least every two weeks to do the following;	
20	Set up service teams within each department or division	
21	Develop Team Vision and Mission	
22	Establish service team goals, roles and responsibilities.	
23	Reinforce values and embed company wide service standards and develop team specific standards if needed.	
24	Have teams assess and strengthen Internal Service Partnerships.	

Conclusion

25	Ensure all team members understand– problem-solving process	
26	Have teams Analyze Moments of Truth and implement changes/improvements.	
27	Develop plan for on-going identification, review and removal of service obstacles.	
28	Develop and implement a plan for continuous service improvement.	
29	Analyze current recovery practices, develop and implement pro-active recovery strategy.	
30	Develop and implement local recognition and reinforcement activities	

Then consistently:

1. Listen
2. Measure
3. Modify
4. Recognize
5. Reward
6. Retrain
7. Communicate
8. Refine
9. Improve

1. Listen
2. Measure
3. Modify
4. Recognize
5. Reward
6. Retrain
7. Communicate
8. Refine
9. Improve

Etc., etc., etc.,

Now That's Customer Focus!

About the Authors

Ray Miller

For the past 20 years Ray has worked with a wide range of
organizations in the development and implementation of customer
focus and training solutions that get results. Ray helps his clients
achieve improved service performance by providing training
solutions that are highly targeted and strategically linked to
operational goals and objectives. The training provided is based on
sound research and employs proven concepts and methodologies
which are delivered in the most appropriate way to achieve the
desired changes in mind-set and performance.

In his past experience Ray has headed the Sales and Service
training group for one of Canada's largest Banks, been training practice leader for the consulting firm
Stevenson Kellogg, President of CanTrain Development Corporation and Managing Partner of The
Training Bank. He has worked with clients, both large and small on training initiatives in Financial
Services, Manufacturing, High Tech, Construction, Aviation, Healthcare and Hospitality industries in
Canada, the United states and abroad. He is a gifted writer and facilitator who has been described as
both knowledgeable, motivational and humorous. Drawing from his extensive business experience,
his focus is on the practical rather than theoretical.

Laura Miller

Laura is a Human Resource Development specialist and Master
Training Designer with over 30 years' experience in research,
design, instruction, and consulting. She has designed and delivered
hundreds of highly effective, training programs, workbooks and self-
study manuals which run the gamut from technical skill
enhancement to management and leadership all of which are linked
to corporate and operational objectives.

Laura is also a gifted writer, speaker and facilitator and has trained
thousands of people Canada and the United States spanning all
ranges from executive management to frontline employees.

In a consulting capacity, Laura has worked with numerous
organizations and business units to define development needs, develop strategies and tactical plans,
design and deliver learning solutions, and evaluate outcomes against objectives.

About the Authors

About our Company

The Training Bank is a full service training and development firm, Headquartered in Toronto, Ontario, Canada.

Operating since 1986, we develop training solutions based on its clients' specific goals and objectives which get results.

We have the ability to provide training solutions in traditional classroom, web-based and blended formats. Our online learning systems and generic programs in service, leadership, relationship selling and coaching are available is many international markets through our distribution network.

While we have developed training in a broad range of subject matter, we have extensive expertise in the realm of customer-focused leadership, customer service and management development. You can find out more about us by visiting our web site at www.trainingbank.com.

Some of our on-site Customer Focus training programs include:
- Customers Forever
- Customer-Focused Leadership
- The Wow Factor

Other eBooks to look for:

That's Customer Focus – The Series
- **Part I – Getting Started**
- **Part II – Building a Strong Foundation**
- **Part III – Learning From the Customer**
- **Part IV – Making it Work**

The Customer Focus Companion

Contact particulars

Email: cantrain@thetrainingbank.com

Website: www.thetrainingbank.com

Telephone: (416) 698-8230

Address: 69 Beech Ave., Toronto, Ontario Canada M4E 3H3